Grammaire créative

by Geneviève Talon

Editor Nicola Lusby
Editorial Manager Teresa Raho
Design Philippa Dalley • Katie Pett
Illustrations Emma Longman • Beehive Illustration

LCP Hampton House • Longfield Road • Leamington Spa • Warwickshire • CV31 1XB
tel: 01926 886914 **fax:** 01926 887136
e-mail: mail@LCPUK.co.uk **website:** www.LCPUK.co.uk

First published 2003

ISBN 1 904178 30 8

Acknowledgements
The author and publisher would like to thank Sarah Haddow and David Jones for their valuable contribution to this publication.

Contents

* (R) = Structures which the QCA flags as 'receptive only' at Foundation Tier.

Introduction

The objective of *Grammaire créative* is systematic presentation and practice of French grammar and linguistic structures. The pack is aimed at young learners in the first three or four years of their course. It is particularly suitable for Key Stage 3 and Foundation Tier students at Key Stage 4, or students in S1 to S4 in Scotland. The choice of structures is based on the QCA list for GCSE Foundation Tier, with additions from the QCA Scheme of Work for Key Stage 3 French. *Grammaire créative* can also be used for quick revision by students preparing for GCSE Higher Tier, or Credit Level in Scotland.

The 87 photocopiable worksheets are all structured in the same way. The grammar or linguistic point is presented as part of a cartoon, designed to be engaging and motivating to students. The explanation which follows draws on examples from the text in the cartoon, and includes exceptions and paradigms, as necessary. The final step is a practice activity which can normally be completed on the sheet itself – only in a very few cases is a separate sheet of paper required. Most of the activities are close-ended, and all the solutions are listed at the back of the book (pages 89–94).

As a good proportion of each sheet is taken up with explanations, including complete paradigms, it is suggested that students put their sheets in a folder for reference, after the activity has been completed and marked. The same applies to the glossary.

Students won't normally need a dictionary to complete the activities, as all the key words should have been made clear in the presentation or in the explanation. The incidental language has been kept as predictable as possible. For instance, all the texts and activities are in the present tense, unless tenses are the grammatical point being tackled.

The worksheets are not numbered in growing order of difficulty, and it should be possible to pick and choose according to the students' needs. However, it would make sense to keep to the order in which they appear within a given topic: for instance, worksheets 21, 22 and 23 all deal with object pronouns, and it would be logical to do 21, *Direct object pronouns*, and 22, *Indirect object pronouns*, before 23, *Order of object pronouns*.

The QCA's list of structures makes a distinction between active knowledge and receptive knowledge for GCSE Foundation Tier, and this is reflected in the *Grammaire créative* activities. Points that are for recognition only do not involve any active production of the structure. They are flagged with (R) on the contents page.

Glossary

Let's call a spade a spade!

Grammar is a way of describing language. Just as the parts of a car all have a name, so the parts of language all have a name too. Grammar terms are a quick and efficient way of naming those parts.

adjective – a describing word: *une voiture rouge, un bon gâteau*

adverb – a word that adds to the meaning of an adjective or a verb: *Max a très chaud.*

to agree – to take an ending that matches a related word in the sentence: *Les petits enfants sont sortis.*

article – a short word in front of a noun; in French, it indicates whether the noun is masculine, feminine or plural: *le/un pull, la/une chaussure, les/des magasins*

auxiliary verb – the verbs *avoir* or *être*, when used to form the perfect tense: *Léo est allé à la piscine et il a nagé.*

cardinal number – the number form used for counting quantities: *un, deux, trois…*

comparative – the form an adjective or an adverb takes when comparing two things or two people: *Thomas est plus grand que Nathalie.*

conditional tense – the tense used to talk about what might happen, and in polite phrases such as *je voudrais.*

definite article – a short word in front of a noun naming something or somebody specific: *le frère, la voiture*

demonstrative (adjective or pronoun) – a small word used to point something out: *Je veux ce livre. Celui-ci? Non, celui-là.*

direct object pronoun – a pronoun that stands for the object of a verb, without a preposition: *Émilie mange une pomme – elle la mange.*

disjunctive pronoun – a pronoun separated from the rest of the sentence by a comma: *Toi, tu es gentil!*

emphatic pronoun – a pronoun that adds emphasis: *C'est lui qui est gentil.*

ending – the last part of a word, which can change: *elle court, elles courent*

feminine – word describing '*la*' nouns and related words: *La voiture bleue est partie.*

future tenses – the tenses used to talk about the future: *Nous allons faire la vaisselle; Nous ferons la vaisselle.*

gender – masculine or feminine quality, which applies to all nouns, not just people: *la chaise, le lit*

imperative – the form of the verb used to give orders or instructions: *Ouvre le livre; Assieds-toi.*

imperfect tense – one tense used to talk about the past, particularly what used to be: *Quand j'étais petit, j'avais un vélo bleu.*

impersonal – said of a verb which hasn't got a specific subject: *il faut, il pleut*

indefinite (article or adjective) – not specific: *un chat, une fleur, chaque professeur*

indefinite article	– a short word in front of a noun naming something or somebody unspecific: *un frère, une voiture, des chevaux*
indirect object pronoun	– a pronoun that stands for a preposition + object of a verb: *Ali téléphone à son père – il lui téléphone.*
infinitive	– the form of the verb you find in the dictionary: *être, partir, se lever*
interrogative (adverb or pronoun)	– said of a word used to ask questions: *Quelle heure est-il?*
invariable	– said of an adjective or noun that never changes (it stays the same in the masculine and the feminine, in the singular and in the plural, etc.): *un train orange, une voiture orange, des fleurs orange; un porte-monnaie, des porte-monnaie*
irregular	– not following the grammatical rule: *aller – je vais*
link word	– a word used to link parts of a sentence: *J'ai un sandwich, mais je n'ai pas faim.*
masculine	– word describing 'le' nouns and related words: *Le train bleu est parti.*
modal verbs	– irregular verbs, such as *vouloir, pouvoir, devoir,* used to indicate intention, possibility, obligation, etc.
negative	– the form words take when saying something is NOT the case: *Camille n'aime pas le chocolat.*
noun	– a label word, for instance *le père, la chaise*
object	– the thing or person that has an action done to it: *Je répare mon vélo; Sophie appelle Théo.*
ordinal number	– the number form used to indicate order: *le premier, le deuxième, le troisième…*
partitive article	– a short word in front of a noun indicating a general quantity: *du thé, des frites*
passive voice	– the form of the verb used to say people or things are having something done to them: *La voiture est réparée par le mécanicien; le mécanicien est payé par le cliént.*
past participle	– the form of the verb used in the perfect tense: *Marine a nagé; Claire est sortie.*
pattern	– the rules followed by the forms of a verb: *je lave, tu laves, il lave, nous lavons, vous lavez, ils lavent*
perfect tense	– one of the tenses used to talk about the past: *Marine a nagé; Claire est sortie.*
personal pronoun	– a pronoun that indicates the subject or object of a verb: *Elles me regardent.*
phrase	– a group of words that doesn't make a complete sentence: *demain matin*
pluperfect tense	– the tense used to talk about what had already happened before a past event: *J'avais fini mes devoirs quand Julien est arrivé.*
plural	– the form words take when talking about several things or people: *Elles vendent des journaux.*
possessive adjective	– an adjective that indicates who owns what: *sa sœur, leur camion*
preposition	– a word locating something in time or space, and often followed by an object: *La classe va à Paris; après les vacances.*
present tense	– the tense used to talk about what's happening now or happens from time to time: *Je fais la vaisselle.*

present participle – the form of the verb used to describe an action happening at the same time as the action of the main verb: *Entendant le téléphone, il est rentré dans la maison.*

pronoun – a short word standing for a noun that has just been used: *Marie est au lit, elle est malade.*

quantifier – a type of adverb indicating a quantity: *un peu, beaucoup*

reflexive – said of a verb which needs two personal pronouns: *je me lève*

regular – following the grammatical rule: *une maison, deux maisons*

relative pronoun – a short word standing for a noun to link two sentences: *Le garçon porte un pull. C'est mon frère. – Le garçon qui porte un pull, c'est mon frère.*

sentence – a group of words, usually including a verb, that make sense together and end with a full stop: *Maintenant, je regarde la télé.*

singular – the form words take when talking about one thing or person: *Le bébé crie.*

stem – the part of a verb that is reused in most of its forms: *j'aime, j'aimais, j'ai aimé, j'aimerai*

subject – the thing or person that does the action indicated by a verb: *Marine fait du vélo.*

superlative – the form an adjective or an adverb takes when comparing a thing or a person with everything else in the category: *Le meilleur coureur, c'est le numéro 24.*

tense – the form a verb takes to say whether something happens in the present, in the past or in the future: *je mange, j'ai mangé, je vais manger*

verb – sometimes called a 'doing' word, it can also describe a state: *Je suis fatigué, alors je vais dormir.*

voice – see **passive**

Articles

- French <u>nouns</u> (label words, such as ***le camion*** or ***la chaise***) are either <u>masculine</u> or <u>feminine</u>.
- When you learn a noun, you have to learn whether it's a masculine noun (*le*/*un*) or a feminine noun (*la*/*une*).
- The <u>definite article</u> (*le, la, les*) is the word for 'the' and the <u>indefinite article</u> (*un, une, des*) is the word for 'a/an', 'some'.
- If the noun starts with a vowel (a, e, i, o, u), *le* or *la* becomes *l'*. It is usually *l'* too if there is an *h* in front of the vowel: ***l'****hôtel*
- In the plural, it is easier: the article is the same (*les* or *des*) for masculine or feminine nouns.
- In English, you can say 'there are tables', without an article, but in French, you always use the indefinite article *des*: *il y a* ***des*** *tables* – 'there are **some** tables'.
- Just like in English, most nouns add an *s* in the plural: *des chaise**s***.

	masculine definite	 indefinite	feminine definite	 indefinite
singular (one only)	***le*** *camion* the lorry	***un*** *camion* a lorry	***la*** *chaise* the chair	***une*** *chaise* a chair
plural (more than one)	***les*** *camion**s*** the lorries	***des*** *camion**s*** lorries	***les*** *chaise**s*** the chairs	***des*** *chaise**s*** chairs

- Madame Martin shows her furniture to Ludovic, the removal man. Fill in the correct <u>definite article</u> (*le/la/les*). To help you, feminine words are underlined and masculine words are circled. But watch out for plural words!

Voici **1.** Exemple ...le... *(piano)*, **2.** .... *(lits)*, **3.** .... *(fauteuils)*,

4. .... *<u>cuisinière</u>*, **5.** .... *(frigo)*, **6.** .... *(lave-vaisselle)*, **7.** .... *<u>armoires</u>*, **8.** .... *(ordinateur)*,

9. .... *(rideaux)*, **10.** .... *<u>moquette</u>*, **11.** .... *<u>étagères</u> et* **12.** .... *<u>baignoire</u>*.

- Now, Ludovic shows his booty to his customers. Fill in the correct <u>indefinite</u> article (*un, une, des*).

Voici **1.** Exemple ...un... *piano*, **2.** .... *lits*, **3.** .... *fauteuils*,

4. .... *cuisinière*, **5.** .... *frigo*, **6.** .... *lave-vaisselle*, **7.** .... *armoires*, **8.** .... *ordinateur*,

9. .... *rideaux*, **10.** .... *moquette*, **11.** .... *étagères et* **12.** .... *baignoire*.

Name:

Nouns

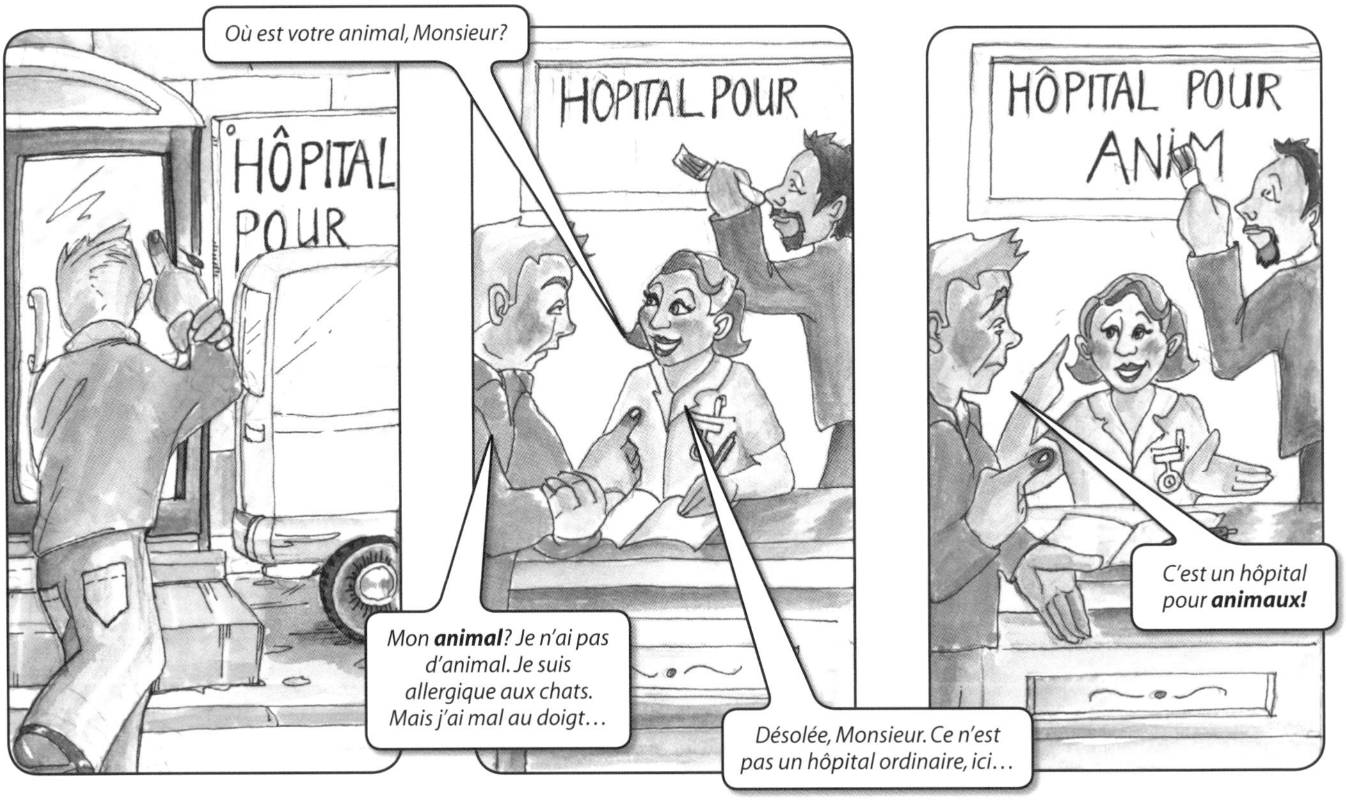

- In the plural, most nouns add an *s*: *les chats*. But there are some exceptions.
- Many words ending in *–al* change their ending to *–aux* in the plural: *un animal, des animaux*.
- Some words ending in *–ail* also change their ending to *–aux* in the plural, which is why the sign for 'roadworks' on French roads reads *travaux* (the plural of *travail*).
- All words ending in *–eau* add an *–x* instead of an *–s*: *un château, des châteaux*.
- A few words ending in *–ou* also add an *–x* instead of an *–s*: *un chou, des choux*.
- Some words ending in *–s*, *–x* or *–z* remain unchanged: *un bois, les bois*.

- Fill in the blanks with the correct plural form.

J'aime beaucoup les (animal) **1.** Exemple *animaux* ...., *surtout les (cheval)* **2.** ....

Mais hier, je suis tombé de cheval, et maintenant j'ai mal aux deux (main) **3.** ....

et aux deux (genou) **4.** .... *. Le docteur a dit: «Il faut aller à l'hôpital. Mais attention:*

il y a plusieurs (hôpital) **5.** .... *dans la ville. Allez à l'hôpital du centre.»*

Dans la salle d'attente de l'hôpital, j'ai lu des (magazine) **6.** ....

et des (journal) **7.** .... *, et j'ai mangé des (gâteau)* **8.** ....

et des (bonbon) **9.** .... *. Ma mère a dit: «La prochaine fois, fais du bateau avec nous.*

Les (bateau) **10.** .... *sont moins dangereux.»*

Dans la salle d'attente, j'ai vu une petite annonce: «L'hôpital cherche des (clown) **11.** .... *, pour*

amuser les (enfant) **12.** .... *malades. S'adresser aux (bureau)* **13.** .... *.»*

C'est bientôt Noël, et je veux acheter des (cadeau) **14.** .... *pour ma famille. J'ai beaucoup*

d' (idée) **15.** .... *, mais pas beaucoup d'argent. Je pourrais travailler comme clown?*

Name:

Partitive article

- The partitive article has the meaning of 'some' or 'any'.
  je voudrais du thé mais je ne veux pas de gâteaux – I'd like some tea but I don't want any cakes
- The partitive article isn't always translated in English: *je voudrais de l'eau* – I'd like (some) water

	masculine	**feminine**	**negative**
singular (one only)	*je voudrais* **du** *thé* (**de l'***alcool*)	*je voudrais* **de la** *limonade* (**de l'***eau*)	*je ne veux pas* **de** *thé*/**de** *limonade*/**d'***eau*
plural (more than one)	*je voudrais* **des** *gâteaux*	*je voudrais* **des** *frites*	*je ne veux pas* **de** *gâteaux*/**de** *frites*

- Fill in the gap with the correct form of the partitive article (*de, de la, du, de l', des*) and the noun.

1. *Je veux envoyer (les lettres)* Exemple *des lettres* – *mais je n'ai pas (les enveloppes)* Exemple *d'enveloppes* .

2. *Je voudrais faire (les crêpes)* .... – *tu as (la farine)* .... ?

3. *Je n'ai pas (les livres)* .... *parce que je n'ai pas (les devoirs)* ....

4. *Dans mon thé, je prends (le lait)* .... *, mais pas (le sucre)* ....

5. *On fait (l'allemand)* .... *et (l'espagnol)* .... ,

mais on ne fait pas (le latin) ....

6. *Il faut (la patience)* .... *et (le courage)* .... *pour ce travail.*

7. *Dans la ville, il y a (les églises)* .... *, mais pas (la cathédrale)* ....

8. *Les végétariens mangent (le fromage)* .... *, mais pas (la viande)* ....

9. *Elle a (l'argent)* .... *, mais elle n'a pas (les amis)* ....

10. *Je cherche (les chaussures)* .... *, mais je ne veux pas (les chaussures)*

.... *chères.*

Name:

Je m'appelle Emily et j'apprends le français. Je voudrais rencontrer un garçon **français**, **cool**, **amusant** et **riche**, avec beaucoup de copains **français**, **cool** et **amusants** (et **riches**).

Agreement of adjectives 1

Je m'appelle Thibaud et j'apprends l'anglais Je voudrais rencontr une fille **anglaise**, **co** **amusante** et **riche**, a beaucoup de copine **anglaises**, **cool** et **amusantes** (et **riches**).

- Adjectives are describing words. Normally, they agree with the noun they describe. If the noun is feminine, they add an *–e*. If the noun is plural, they add an *–s*.

	masculine	**feminine**
singular **plural**	*un garçon amusant* *des garçons amusant**s***	*une fille amusant**e*** *des filles amusant**es***

- But there are some exceptions:
  Adjectives that already end with *–e*, like *riche*, don't add an extra *–e* in the feminine.
  Adjectives that already end with *–s*, like *français*, don't add an extra *–s* in the masculine plural.
  Some adjectives, often those with a slang meaning, don't change at all and are invariable: *des filles cool*.

	masculine	**feminine**
singular	*riche* *français* *cool*	*riche* *français**e*** *cool*
plural	*riche**s*** *français* *cool*	*riche**s*** *français**es*** *cool*

vacances ***f***
paysages ***m***
villes ***f***
Écossais ***m***
visiteurs ***m***
plages ***f***

- Fill in the blanks with the correct form of the adjective. Watch out for gender: are the nouns masculine or feminine?

Pour vos (prochain) **1.** ....Exemple prochaines.... *vacances, visitez l'Écosse! C'est la destination (idéal)*

2. .... *. Les paysages (écossais)* **3.** .... *sont (vert)*

4. .... *et (varié)* **5.** .... *et les villes (écossais)*

6. .... *, comme Édimbourg et Glasgow, sont très (élégant)* **7.** ....

Et bien sûr, les Écossais sont très (sympa) **8.** .... *et ils aiment beaucoup les visiteurs (français)*

9. .... *. Vous pouvez visiter un (vrai)* **10.** .... *château (hanté)*

11. .... *et voir des plages (propre)* **12.** .... *et pas (pollué)*

13. .... *. Pour les transports, il y a une solution (simple)* **14.** .... *et*

(pratique) **15.** .... *, l'avion.*

Name:

Agreement of adjectives 2

- Adjectives are describing words. Normally, they agree with the noun they describe. If the noun is feminine, they add an *–e*. If the noun is plural, they add an *–s*.

	masculine	feminine
singular	*un manteau élégant*	*une robe élégante*
plural	*des manteaux élégants*	*des robes élégantes*

- But there are some exceptions:
  The ending *–ien* becomes *–ienne* in the feminine: *canadien, canadienne.*
  The ending *–eux* becomes *–euse* in the feminine, and doesn't change in the masculine plural: *un château affreux, une maison affreuse, des châteaux affreux.*
  Some adjectives are irregular and you have to learn the feminine and plural forms by heart:

masculine singular	feminine singular	masculine plural	feminine plural
beau	*belle*	*beaux*	*belles*
blanc	*blanche*	*blancs*	*blanches*
bon	*bonne*	*bons*	*bonnes*
cher	*chère*	*chers*	*chères*
faux	*fausse*	*faux*	*fausses*
gentil	*gentille*	*gentils*	*gentilles*
gros	*grosse*	*gros*	*grosses*
long	*longue*	*longs*	*longues*
neuf	*neuve*	*neufs*	*neuves*
nouveau	*nouvelle*	*nouveaux*	*nouvelles*
vieux	*vieille*	*vieux*	*vieilles*

repas **m**
tables **f**
chaises **f**
option **f**
portion **f**
desserts **m**

- Maeva gives her opinion about the school canteen. Fill in the blanks with the correct form of the adjective. Watch out for gender: are the nouns masculine or feminine?

On a une (nouveau) **1.** Exemple: nouvelle *cantine à l'école. (L' (ancien)* **2.** .... *cantine était (affreux)* **3.** .... *), mais les repas sont toujours aussi (ennuyeux)* **4.** .... *. Les tables sont (neuf)* **5.** .... *, c'est vrai, et les chaises (blanc)* **6.** .... *sont assez (beau)* **7.** .... *. Malheureusement, la cuisine n'est pas (bon)* **8.** .... *. Les cuisinières sont (gentil)* **9.** .... *, mais elles sont plutôt (paresseux)* **10.** .... *. L'option (végétarien)* **11.** .... *, par exemple, c'est toujours la même chose: une omelette. En plus, les portions ne sont pas assez (gros)* **12.** .... *. L'exception, c'est les desserts: ils sont (délicieux)* **13.** .... *. Aujourd'hui, je suis (heureux)* **14.** .... *: il y a du tiramisu!*

Name:

Position of adjectives

- In French, adjectives (describing words) normally come after the noun: *un vin rouge, un restaurant français.*
- A few adjectives come before the noun: *un grand vin, un bon restaurant.* Here is a list:

autre/autre – other	*gentil/gentille* – kind	*joli/jolie* – pretty
beau/belle – beautiful	*grand/grande* – great	*long/longue* – long
bon/bonne – good	*gros/grosse* – big	*mauvais/mauvaise* – bad
court/courte – short	*haut/haute* – high	*petit/petite* – small, little
dernier/dernière – last	*jeune/jeune* – young	*vieux/vieille* – old

- The meaning of some adjectives varies according to their position. Here are three examples:

***cher** Papa* – dear Daddy	*une montre **chère*** – an expensive watch
*mon **ancien** vélo* – my previous bike	*une maison **ancienne*** – an old house
*ma **propre** chambre* – my own bedroom	*une chambre **propre*** – a clean bedroom

- Remember that when the adjective comes first, the article *des* is replaced with *de*:
  Je voudrais des pommes.
  Je voudrais de grosses pommes.

- Émilie is on holiday with a friend's family. Read the letter and write the adjective before or after the noun as appropriate

1.	Exemple: Chère *Maman*	*chère*
2.	*Je passe de* .... *vacances* .... *à Juan-les-Bains.*	*bonnes*
3.	*C'est une* .... *ville*	*agréable*
4.	*Il y a une* .... *plage*	*propre*
5.	*Le matin, je fais de* .... *promenades*	*longues*
6.	*L'après-midi, nous allons dans les cafés du* .... *port*	*vieux*
7.	*Ou nous faisons des courses dans les* .... *boutiques*	*jolies*
8.	*Les boutiques vendent surtout des* .... *vêtements*	*chers*
9.	*Par contre, les cinémas passent des* .... *films*	*ennuyeux*
10.	*Le soir, nous faisons de* .... *repas*	*bons*
11.	*Nous avons un* .... *appartement*	*petit*
12.	*C'est un* .... *appartement*	*ancien*
13.	*Je n'ai pas ma* .... *chambre* .... *: je partage avec Lucie.*	*propre*
14.	*Lucie a une* .... *famille*	*sympa*
15.	*Oui, ce sont des* .... *vacances*	*fantastiques*

Name:

Comparatives

- Adjectives in the comparative are used to compare two things.
  *Le lapin est **plus** rapide **que** le chat.* (+) – The rabbit is fast**er than** the cat.
  *Le chat est **aussi** rapide **que** le grizzli.* (=) – The cat is **as** fast **as** the grizzly bear.
  *Le grizzli est **moins** rapide **que** le lapin.* (–) – The grizzly bear is **less** fast **than** the rabbit.
- Just like in English, the comparative of the adjective *bon* (good) is irregular:
  *Le gâteau au chocolat est **meilleur que** le brocoli.* – Chocolate cake is **better than** broccoli.

- Write a sentence with a comparative.

1. *le mont Blanc / haut / Ben Nevis* +

Exemple Le mont Blanc est plus haut que Ben Nevis.

2. *le mont Blanc / haut / l'Everest* –

3. *le pingouin / rapide / le saumon* =

4. *le Shinkansen (un train japonais) / rapide / le TGV (un train français)* +

5. *le Flying Scotsman / rapide / le TGV* –

6. *une Ferrari / chère / une Rolls-Royce* =

7. *en ski, les Norvégiens / bons / les Espagnols* +

8. *la France / grande / la Grande-Bretagne* +

9. *la Grande-Bretagne / grande / les États-Unis* –

10. *l'espagnol / difficile / le français* =

11. *le climat en Italie / chaud / le climat en Irlande* +

12. *le climat en Islande / chaud / le climat en Irlande* –

13. *le tigre sibérien / rare / le panda* =

14. *en base-ball, le Canada / bon / la France* +

Name:

Superlatives

- Adjectives in the superlative are used to compare something with everything else in its category.
  Note how in French you use the article twice: once in front of the noun, once in front of the adjective.
  la *voiture* ***la plus*** *chère du monde* – the most expensive car in the world
- However, if the adjective is one of those that comes before the noun (*beau, bon, court, gentil, grand, gros, haut, jeune, joli, long, mauvais, petit, vieux*), you only use the article once:
  le plus *vieux vélo du magasin* – the oldest bike in the shop
- Note that you say ***du*** *monde* for 'in the world', ***de la*** *classe* for 'in the class', etc.
- Just as in English, the superlative of the adjective *bon* (good) is irregular:
  Le meilleur *chocolat, c'est le chocolat belge.* – **The best** chocolate is Belgian chocolate.

- Write a sentence with a superlative. Watch out for adjectives that come before the noun.

1. *le guépard / l'animal / rapide* +
   Exemple: Le guépard est l'animal le plus rapide.
2. *le bateau / le moyen de transport / dangereux* –
3. *le vin français / le vin / bon / Europe* +
4. *Harry Potter / le livre pour enfants / célèbre* +
5. *en Écosse, on trouve les plages / polluées / Grande-Bretagne* –
6. *le colibri / l'oiseau / petit / monde* +
7. *le train / le moyen de transport / fatigant* –
8. *la reine Elizabeth / la femme / importante / Angleterre* +
9. *l'autruche / l'oiseau / intelligent* –
10. *Sydney / la ville / grande / Australie* +
11. *les élèves préfèrent les professeurs / sévères* –
12. *Jéricho / la ville / ancienne / monde* +

Name:

Demonstrative adjectives

- The demonstrative adjective *ce* means 'this' or 'that', and it changes according to the nouns that follows. With a masculine noun, you use *ce* (*cet* if it starts with a vowel). With a feminine noun, you use *cette*. *Ces* is the plural form: it means 'these' or 'those'.
  Je voudrais cet anorak. – I would like this jacket.
  Je voudrais ces gants. – I would like those gloves.

masculine	**masculine** (word starting with a vowel or an *h*)	**feminine**	**plural**
ce *pantalon*	***cet*** *anorak/****cet*** *hôtel*	***cette*** *écharpe*	***ces*** *gants*

- Complete the sentences with these words, using the correct demonstrative adjective.

A *un appareil-photo*
une caméra
des téléphones portables
un ordinateur

1. *Je voudrais* Exemple cet appareil-photo .
2. *Je voudrais* ....
3. *Je voudrais* ....
4. *Je voudrais* ....

B *un immeuble*
des maisons
une église
un château

1. *J'ai visité* ....
2. *J'ai visité* ....
3. *J'ai visité* ....
4. *J'ai visité* ....

C *des graffiti*
un incendie
un accident
un orage

1. *J'ai vu* ....
2. *J'ai vu* ....
3. *J'ai vu* ....
4. *J'ai vu* ....

D *une pomme*
des raisins
un melon
un abricot

1. *Tu veux* .... ?
2. *Tu veux* .... ?
3. *Tu veux* .... ?
4. *Tu veux* .... ?

Name:

Indefinite adjectives

- *Chaque* and *quelques* are adjectives which mean 'each' and 'some':
  ***Chaque** Zylbek est différent.* – Each Zylbeck is different.
  ***Quelques** Zylbeks sont explorateurs.* – Some Zylbeks are explorers.
- Note these three useful phrases:
  quelqu'un means 'somebody', *quelques-uns* 'some of them' and *quelque chose* 'something'.
  *Voici **quelqu'un**.* – Here is somebody.
  ***Quelques-uns** sont sportifs.* – Some of them like sport.
  *Chaque Zylbeck fait **quelque chose** de différent.* – Each Zylbeck does something different.

* *le moniteur* – youth leader

- Cyril is spending a holiday at a *camp d'ados*, a summer camp for teenagers. He writes to his grandmother. Fill in the blanks with *chaque, quelques, quelqu'un, quelques-uns* or *quelque chose*.

Chère Grand-mère

Comme **1.** Exemple chaque *année, je passe de bonnes vacances au camp d'ados. Il y a 40 ados de 14 à 17 ans.*

C'est confortable: **2.** .... *ado a sa tente.*

Les ados sont sympa, en général. **3.** .... *sont musiciens. Kévin joue du clavier, par exemple.*

4. .... *jeunes ont aussi une guitare.*

5. .... *moniteur* est responsable d'un groupe de six ou sept ados.* **6.** .... *moniteurs sont étrangers: il y a deux Anglais et un Irlandais.* **7.** .... *groupe fait la cuisine une fois par semaine. Si* **8.** .... *ne veut pas faire la cuisine, il (ou elle) fait la vaisselle.*

C'est intéressant, parce qu'il y a toujours **9.** .... *à faire. Pour les activités, on décide ensemble.*

Si **10.** .... *veut faire de l'équitation, par exemple, il propose l'activité au moniteur. Il y a aussi* **11.** .... *vélos au camp: c'est pratique pour faire les courses. Si on veut* **12.** .... *dans un magasin, on prend un vélo.*

À bientôt, Grand-mère. Je t'embrasse.

Cyril

Name:

Possessive adjectives 1

* *à la fourrière* – (towed away) to the car pound

There is more than one word in French for 'my'. To decide which one to use, you need to know whether the thing you own is masculine or feminine. The same applies to 'your' when talking to a friend or a young person, and to 'his', 'her', 'its'. What matters is whether the thing owned is masculine or feminine, NOT whether the owner is male or female.

	masculine thing	**feminine thing**	**feminine thing** (word starting with a vowel)
my your (to a friend or a young person) his/her/its	*un vélo – **mon** vélo* *un vélo – **ton** vélo* *un vélo – **son** vélo*	*une moto – **ma** moto* *une moto – **ta** moto* *une moto – **sa** moto*	*une auto – **mon** auto* *une auto – **ton** auto* *une auto – **son** auto*

- In English, when you hear 'his bike', you know the bike belongs to a boy or a man.
  In French, when you hear *son vélo*, you don't know whether it belongs to a boy or a girl, a man or a woman – all you know is that *vélo* is a masculine (*le*) noun.
- It is easier when the thing has several owners. Then you need only one word for 'our', one word for 'your' (talking to several people or to an unfamiliar adult) and one word for 'their'.

	singular (single object)
our your (to a group of people, or to an unfamiliar adult) their	***notre** auto* ***votre** auto* ***leur** auto*

amie **f**	*musique* **f**
mère **f**	*anniversaire* **m**
ordinateur **m**	*restaurant* **m**
chambre **f**	*copine* **f**
duvet **m**	*lit* **m**

- Jade wants to invite her friend Émilie for the weekend, but Jade shares a room with her older sister Stéphanie, who isn't keen on Émilie staying with them.
  Fill in the blanks in the dialogue with *mon, ma, ton, ta, son, sa, notre, votre* or *leur*.
  Watch out for gender: are the nouns masculine or feminine?

Jade: *Je voudrais inviter* **1.** (Exemple) mon *amie, Émilie, ce week-end.* **2.** .... *mère part en voyage. On voudrait écouter de la musique sur* **3.** .... *ordinateur.*

Stéphanie: *Mais* **4.** .... *chambre est trop petite! Il y a seulement deux lits.*

Jade: *Émilie peut apporter* **5.** .... *duvet et dormir sur le canapé du séjour.*

Stéphanie: *Et puis, je n'aime pas* **6.** .... *musique, à Émilie et à toi. Elle n'est pas cool.* **7.** .... *musique, c'est mieux.*

Jade: **8.** .... *musique est aussi cool que* **9.** .... *musique!*

Stéphanie: *Et Papa et Maman? C'est* **10.** .... *anniversaire de mariage samedi.*

Jade: *Justement, ils vont dans* **11.** .... *restaurant préféré.*

Stéphanie: *Bon, invite* **12.** .... *copine si tu veux, mais moi, j'invite* **13.** .... *copine Céleste. Elle peut dormir dans la salle de bains.*

Jade: *Ou dans* **14.** .... *lit, et toi, tu dors dans la salle de bains!*

Name:

Possessive adjectives 2

- Talking about several things that 'belong' is simpler than talking about one thing: you don't have to worry about the gender (masculine or feminine) of the noun.

	plural noun
my	***mes*** *notes*
your (to a friend or a young person)	***tes*** *notes*
his/her/its	***ses*** *notes*
our	***nos*** *notes*
your (to a group of people, or to one unfamiliar adult)	***vos*** *notes*
their	***leurs*** *notes*

Mes *notes sont mauvaises.* – **My** marks are low.
Ses *explications ne sont pas claires.* – **His/Her** explanations are not clear.
Leurs *profs sont sévères.* – **Their** teachers are strict.

- Class 3B are on a skiing and outdoors trip. They're having some problems finding their equipment. Read the dialogues and fill in the blanks with possessive adjectives.

1. **Prof:** Exemple *Vos* .... *chaussures sont dans le placard.*
   Élèves 1 & 2: *Et* .... *gants?*
   Prof: .... *gants aussi.*
2. **Prof:** *Carl n'est pas là?*
   Élève 1: *Non, il a perdu* .... *skis dans la neige.*
3. **Élève 1:** *Je ne trouve pas* .... *patins à roulettes!*
   Prof: .... *patins à roulettes sont dans la valise.*
4. **Prof:** *Où sont Martin et Sophie?*
   Élève 1: *Dans la maison. Ils cherchent* .... *lunettes.*
5. **Élève 1:** *J'ai* .... *baskets, mais où sont* .... *raquettes?*
   Élèves 2 & 3: *Nos raquettes sont dans le sac, avec* .... *balles.*
6. **Prof:** *Apportez* .... *CD, pour écouter de la musique le soir.*
   Élève: *Oui, Yussef et Amina apportent* .... *CD.*
7. **Pierre:** *Madame, Louis a* .... *skis!*
   Prof: *Louis, redonne* .... *skis à Pierre.*

Name:

Comparative and superlative adverbs

- An <u>adverb</u> changes the meaning of a verb or an adjective:
  Sophie parle ***mal*** *l'anglais.* – Sophie speaks English **badly**.
- An adverb, like an adjective, can be used in the comparative or the superlative.
  Jérémie parle l'anglais ***plus mal que*** *Sophie.* – Jérémie speaks English **worse than** Sophie.
  Mais c'est Aurélie qui parle ***le plus mal****.* – But it's Aurélie who speaks it **worst**.
- The adverb *bien* is irregular in the comparative and in the superlative:
  Paul conduit ***bien****.* – Paul drives **well**.
  Paul conduit ***mieux****.* – Paul drives **better**.
  C'est Paul qui conduit ***le mieux****.* – It's Paul who drives **best**.
  Marion conduit ***moins*** *bien que Paul.* – Marion doesn't drive as well as Paul.

- Fill in the blanks in the sentences first with a comparative, then with a superlative.

1. *Renaud habite près du collège.*

Sonia habite + ... Exemple: plus près que .... *Renaud.*

Mais c'est Joanne qui habite + ... Exemple: le plus près ....

2. *L'Airbus vole vite.*

Le Boeing 707 vole + ... *l'Airbus.*

Mais c'est le Boeing 747 qui vole + ...

3. *Jeanne ne sort pas souvent le soir.*

Kévin sort – .... *Jeanne.*

Mais c'est Simon qui sort – ....

4. *Sylvain joue bien de la guitare.*

Caroline joue + ... *Sylvain.*

Mais c'est Christelle qui joue + ...

5. *Tours n'est pas loin de Paris.*

Reims est – .... *Tours.*

Mais c'est Orléans qui est – ....

6. *Les légumes poussent facilement dans ce jardin.*

Les fleurs poussent + ... *les légumes.*

Mais c'est l'herbe qui pousse + ...

Name:

Interrogative adverbs

- Here are some useful question words:
  Quand *part le prochain train?* – **When** does the next train leave?
  Combien de temps *dure le voyage?* – **How long** is the journey?
  Où *va ce train?* – **Where** does this train go?
  Pourquoi *es-tu en retard?* – **Why** are you late?
  Combien *coûte le billet?* – **How much** is the ticket?
  À quelle heure *part le bus?* – **What time** does the bus leave?
  Comment *s'écrit ce mot?* – **How** do you spell this word?

- An old lady, Madame Leriche, has been murdered, and all her money taken. Inspector Clozou questions Damien Lebandit, a suspect.
  Fill in the correct question word.

1. - Exemple: Comment .... *vous appelez-vous?*
- Je m'appelle Damien Lebandit.

2. - .... *habitez-vous?*
- À Paris, au 16, rue Levallois.

3. - .... *êtes-vous allé hier soir?*
- Je suis allé chez Madame Leriche.

4. - .... *êtes-vous allé chez Madame Leriche?*
- Pour réparer sa télévision.

5. - .... *êtes-vous arrivé chez Madame Leriche?*
- À 6 heures.

6. - .... *êtes-vous resté avec Madame Leriche?*
- 30 minutes, c'est tout.

7. - .... *êtes-vous rentré chez vous?*
- Immédiatement.

8. - .... *êtes-vous rentré chez vous?*
- Je suis rentré en voiture.

9. - .... *d'argent avez-vous demandé à Madame Leriche?*
- 50 euros. C'est le prix normal, pour réparer une télévision.

10. - .... *gagnez-vous par mois?*
- 2000 euros.

11. - *Alors,* .... *avez-vous 50 000 euros à la banque?*

Name:

Adverbs of time

- The words in bold in the cartoon are adverbs of time.
  You need them to say when something happened or will happen.

aujourd'hui – today
d'abord – first
de bonne heure – early
déjà – already
demain – tomorrow
en même temps – at the same time
en retard – late
enfin – finally
ensuite – then
hier – yesterday
récemment – recently
plus tard – later
tard – late
tôt – early
tout de suite – straight away

- Madame Servan is back from her conference – and she isn't happy! This is what she tells Thomas.
  Look at the underlined adverbs and circle the adverb which makes most sense.

Exemple

1. *(Hier) / Demain, je me suis levée* **2.** *d'abord / tôt et j'ai travaillé dur, mais toi, tu t'es levé* **3.** *tard / ensuite et tu n'as rien fait!*

4. *De bonne heure / Aujourd'hui, c'est différent ...*

5. *D'abord / Hier, range ta chambre et fais ton lit.*

6. *En même temps / En retard, cherche tes chaussures de sport: je suis sûre qu'elles sont dans ta chambre.*

7. *De bonne heure / Ensuite, fais tes devoirs. Tu as eu de mauvaises notes en maths* **8.** *récemment / demain, et tes devoirs sont souvent* **9.** *en retard / plus tard. Il faut travailler plus.*

10. *Tôt / Plus tard, tu vas laver la voiture.*

Si tu fais tout ton travail, tu peux **11.** *d'abord / enfin regarder la télé.*

12. *Hier / Demain, tu te lèves* **13.** *déjà / de bonne heure et tu vas nettoyer le jardin.*

Allez, au travail, **14.** *plus tard / tout de suite. Il est* **15.** *déjà / ensuite midi!*

Name:

Adverbs of frequency

- The words in bold in the cartoon are <u>adverbs of time</u>. You need these particular adverbs to say how often something takes place.

encore – again	*ne...jamais* – not ever/never	*souvent* – often
en général – in general	*parfois* – sometimes	*toujours* – always
généralement – generally	*quelquefois* – sometimes	*tous les jours* – every day

- Read about Jack, Djamila and Carmen's eating habits, and fill the gaps with an adverb. There can be several correct answers, but choose the most logical one.

Jack mange équilibré; il n'est pas végétarien.

Moi, je mange des fruits et des légumes **1.** Exemple tous les jours **2.** Exemple Quelquefois, *je mange du poulet ou du poisson. Je ne mange* **3.** .... *de burgers ou de frites.*

4. .... *, je bois de l'eau, mais* **5.** .... *je bois du jus de fruits ou du thé.*

Djamila ne mange pas de viande. Elle mange un peu de poisson, mais surtout elle aime bien les desserts et les choses sucrées.

Moi, je ne mange **6.** .... *de bifteck.* **7.** .... *, je mange du poisson. À la cantine, je choisis* **8.** .... *un fruit, et* **9.** .... *un gâteau. Chez moi, j'ai* **10.** .... *des bonbons sur mon bureau.*

Carmen ne mange pas équilibré.

À midi, à la cantine, je choisis **11.** .... *les frites. À la sortie de l'école, j'achète* **12.** .... *du chocolat. Le soir, je mange* **13.** .... *des frites.*

Avant de me coucher, je prends **14.** .... *un biscuit, ou* **15.** .... *du chocolat. Par contre, je ne mange* **16.** .... *de salade ou de fruits.*

Name:

Adverbs of place

- The words in bold in the cartoon are <u>adverbs</u>. You need these particular adverbs to say <u>where</u> something takes place.
- Be careful with *là*, which can mean 'here' as well as 'there':
  Il n'est pas là. – He isn't here.

en plein air – in the open	*par ici* – this way
ici – here	*par là* – that way
là – here, there	*par terre* – on the ground
là-bas – over there	*partout* – everywhere
loin – far (away)	*près* – near

- Match each French sentence to the correct English sentence.
  Beware: there is always one English sentence too many.

A
1. *Le spectacle est en plein air.* Exemple: C
2. *Le spectacle est par ici.* ☐
3. *Le spectacle est loin.* ☐

a) The show is far away.
b) The show is near.
c) The show is in the open.
d) The show is this way.

B
1. *Les jouets sont par terre.* ☐
2. *Les jouets sont par là.* ☐
3. *Les jouets sont partout.* ☐

a) The toys are everywhere.
b) The toys are far away.
c) The toys are over there.
d) The toys are on the ground.

C
1. *Les brochures sont ici.* ☐
2. *Les brochures sont là-bas.* ☐
3. *Les brochures sont par terre.* ☐

a) The brochures are this way.
b) The brochures are on the ground.
c) The brochures are over there.
d) The brochures are here.

D
1. *Les cars de touristes sont là.* ☐
2. *Les cars de touristes sont partout.* ☐
3. *Les cars de touristes sont près.* ☐

a) The tourist coaches are everywhere.
b) The tourist coaches are here.
c) The tourist coaches are that way.
d) The tourist coaches are near.

Name:

depuis and il y a

* *la tempête* – storm
* *a coulé* – sank

Here are two ways of talking about the past:

- To talk about a state begun a while ago, but not finished yet, you use *depuis* and the present tense.
  This is different from the English, where you use 'for' (with a duration) or 'since' (with a starting point) and the past tense.
  Je suis ici ***depuis*** *20 ans.* (present tense) – I have been here **for** 20 years. (past tense)
  Je suis ici ***depuis*** *la grande tempête.* (present tense) – I have been here **since** the big storm. (past tense)
- If you want to talk about an event which happened a while ago, and which might or might not be finished, you use the phrase *il y a* to translate 'ago'.
  You use a past tense, just like in English, but watch out for the position of *il y a*.
  Mon bateau a coulé ***il y a*** *20 ans.* – My boat sank 20 years **ago**.
  Je suis arrivé sur l'île ***il y a*** *20 ans.* – I arrived on the island 20 years **ago**.
  The important thing to remember is that the events (boat sank, arrived) are over, even though you are still stuck on the island!

- Make up logical sentences, using *il y a* and *depuis*.

1. *Damien – habiter à Paris – 1995*
   Exemple: Damien habite à Paris depuis 1995.
2. *Lucie – casser sa montre – trois jours*
   Exemple: Lucie a cassé sa montre il y a trois jours.
3. *le 1er janvier – Benjamin – faire de la natation*
4. *Natacha – apprendre l'allemand – deux ans*
5. *deux mois – Valentin – visiter la National Gallery*
6. *2002 – Juliette – faire de la danse*
7. *Pablo – acheter une moto – un an*
8. *Léa – faire de l'équitation – cinq ans*
9. *Djamel – vivre en France – 1999*
10. *six mois – Sophie – aller à Disneyland Paris*
11. *Adrien – habiter chez son père – deux ans*
12. *une semaine – Lauren – perdre son portable*

Name:

Quantifiers

- You use words like *un peu, assez, beaucoup, très, trop* to talk about quantity (how much, how many) or about intensity (how strongly you feel about something). You can use them with a verb (*j'aime* in the examples), a noun (*la neige* in the examples), an adjective (*froid* in the examples).
- Note that with a verb, the quantifier goes straight after the verb: *J'aime **trop** le ski.* – I like skiing **too much**.

with a verb:	with a noun:	with an adjective:
j'aime le ski I like skiing	*il y a de la neige* there is some snow	*il fait froid* it is cold
*j'aime **un peu** le ski* I like skiing **a little**	*il y a **un peu de** neige* there is **a little** snow	*il fait **un peu** froid* it is **a little** cold
*j'aime **assez** le ski* I **quite** like skiing	*il y a **assez de** neige* there is **enough** snow	*il fait **assez** froid* it is **quite** cold
*j'aime **beaucoup** le ski* I like skiing **a lot** *(je n'aime **pas beaucoup** le ski* **I don't much** like skiing)	*il y a **beaucoup de** neige* there is **a lot of** snow *(il n'y a **pas beaucoup de neige*** there **isn't a lot of** snow)	*il fait **très** froid* it is **very** cold *(il ne fait **pas très** froid* it **isn't very** cold)
*j'aime **trop** le ski* I like skiing **too much**	*il y a **trop de** neige* there is **too much** snow	*il fait **trop** froid* it is **too** cold

- Fill in the blanks with the most logical words, one word per blank.

1. *Je n'aime pas cette soupe: il y a* Exemple trop *de sel.*
2. *Le dimanche matin, il n'y a* Exemple pas beaucoup *de voitures sur la route.*
3. *Il pleut* .... *: prends ton parapluie.*
4. *Il pleut* .... *: je ne sors pas!*
5. *Le cours de photographie est annulé: il n'y a* .... *de participants.*
6. *Si tu as* .... *chaud, enlève ton pull.*
7. *L'hiver en Tunisie, il ne fait* .... *froid: on peut se baigner.*
8. *Ahmed est* .... *malade, mais ce n'est pas grave: il va à l'école.*
9. *Saïda est* .... *malade pour aller à l'école.*
10. *Baptiste est à l'hôpital aujourd'hui, parce qu'il est* .... *malade.*
11. *Le lundi matin, il y a* .... *de voitures sur la route.*
12. *Le lundi matin, il y a* .... *de voitures sur la route, alors je prends le train.*
13. *J'aime* .... *la physique, mais je préfère les maths: j'aime* .... *l'algèbre.*
14. *Il est mauvais, ton gâteau: il n'y a* .... *de sucre.*

Name:

Relative pronouns

- The <u>relative pronoun</u> *qui* is the <u>subject</u> of the verb that follows: it stands for the person or thing that does the action. In English, it is translated as 'who', 'which' or 'that'. In this example, the mice are doing the eating:
  Je déteste ces souris ***<u>qui</u> mangent*** *mon fromage.* – I hate those mice **<u>that</u> eat** my cheese.
- The relative pronoun *que* is the object of the verb that follows: it stands for the person or thing that is having the action done to them. In English, it is translated as 'who(m)', 'which' or 'that', or sometimes as nothing at all.
  In this example, the mice are being eaten:
  Ces souris ***<u>que</u> je mange*** *sont délicieuses.* – These mice **(<u>that</u>) I am eating** are delicious.
- In front of a vowel or an *h* followed by a vowel, *que* becomes *qu'*:
  Ces souris ***<u>qu'</u>il mange*** *sont délicieuses.* – These mice **(<u>that</u>) he is eating** are delicious.

- For each French sentence, tick the English sentence which is closer in meaning.

Exemple

1. *La guitare que je veux est trop chère.*
   a) There's a guitar which is too expensive for me. ☑
   b) I want to buy an expensive guitar. ☐
2. *Je voudrais un ami qui aime le rap et le hip-hop.*
   a) I'd like to play rap and hip-hop with a friend. ☐
   b) I want a friend who likes rap and hip-hop. ☐
3. *Voici le CD qu'elle préfère.*
   a) This is her favourite CD. ☐
   b) Here is the CD I'd like for her. ☐
4. *Mon amie, qui est italienne, chante dans un groupe.*
   a) My Italian friend sings in a group. ☐
   b) My friend sings in an Italian group. ☐
5. *L'instrument que j'aime le moins, c'est l'accordéon.*
   a) The accordion is my least favourite instrument. ☐
   b) I like this instrument less than the accordion. ☐
6. *Ma mère, qui a 50 ans, aime beaucoup danser.*
   a) My mother has liked dancing for 50 years. ☐
   b) My mother likes dancing, and she is 50. ☐
7. *Le chatroom que je recommande s'appelle MusicFrance.*
   a) I was recommended a chatroom called MusicFrance. ☐
   b) I recommend a chatroom called MusicFrance. ☐
8. *La chanson qu'elle a choisie est la meilleure.*
   a) She chose the best song. ☐
   b) The song chosen for her is the best. ☐
9. *Je cherche un professeur de batterie qui n'habite pas trop loin.*
   a) My drum teacher lives too far away. ☐
   b) I'd like a drum teacher who lives nearby. ☐
10. *Le DJ que je veux entendre, c'est Laurent Garnier.*
    a) Laurent Garnier is the DJ I'd like to listen to. ☐
    b) I'd like to hear Laurent Garnier and a DJ. ☐
11. *Ma sœur, qui a 16 ans, préfère l'opéra.*
    a) My sister has liked opera for 16 years. ☐
    b) My 16-year-old sister likes opera best. ☐
12. *Mon ami Édouard, qui a beaucoup d'argent, a acheté un piano.*
    a) My friend Édouard has bought an expensive piano. ☐
    b) My friend Édouard has bought a piano – he has a lot of money. ☐

Name:

Direct object pronouns

* *vider* – to empty
* *je jette* – I throw away
* *je garde* – I keep
* *Emmaüs* – charity like Oxfam

- The words in bold are <u>direct object pronouns</u>. They look like definite articles, but they replace the noun which has just been talked about: *je **la** jette* – I throw it away.
- Just like the articles, the direct object pronouns *le* and *la* become *l'* in front of a vowel (*a, e, i, o, u*): *je **l'**aime bien* – I like it.

- What will Aurélie's grandmother do with the rest of the clothes? Write the name in the correct column.

1. ***la chemise*** *le pull* *les chaussures*
   Je la donne à Emmaüs. *Je le garde.* *Je les jette.*
2. *les baskets* *le chapeau* *la veste*
   Je la garde. *Je les donne à Emmaüs.* *Je le jette.*
3. *le bonnet* *les collants* *la ceinture*
   Je la jette. *Je les garde.* *Je le donne à Emmaüs.*
4. *le blouson* *les chaussettes* *la jupe*
   Je la donne à Emmaüs. *Je les jette, mais ça, je l'aime.*
5. *le T-shirt* *la casquette* *les gants*
   Je la jette. *Je le donne à Emmaüs.* *Je les garde.*

	jeter	***aimer/garder***	***donner à Emmaüs***
1.	....	....	Exemple la chemise
2.	....	....	....
3.	....	....	....
4.	....	....	....
5.	....	....	....

Name:

Indirect object pronouns

- The words in bold are <u>indirect object pronouns</u>.
  They replace nouns after verbs followed by *à*, such as:
  *expliquer **à** quelqu'un* – to explain to someone
  *téléphoner **à** quelqu'un* – to phone someone
  *parler **à** quelqu'un* – to talk to someone
  *(r)apporter **à** quelqu'un* – to bring (back) to someone
  *acheter **à** quelqu'un* – to buy for someone
  *donner **à** quelqu'un* – to give to someone etc.

  *Alors, je **vous** explique.* – So, let me explain **to you**.
  *Je ne **leur** parle pas.* – I don't speak **to them**.

to me	*me*
to you	*te* (talking to one friend or family member)
to him/to her	*lui*
to us	*nous*
to you	*vous*
to them	*leur*

- Note that the same pronoun, *lui*, is used for a man/a boy and a girl/a woman.
  *Je ne **lui** parle pas.* – I don't speak **to him/to her**.

- Read what Chloé Joubert says about her mother. Then tick the sentences that are correct.
  The first one has been done for you.

Ma mère voyage beaucoup pour son travail. Quand elle est en voyage, elle nous téléphone tous les jours.
Elle nous parle longtemps. Quand elle revient, elle nous rapporte des cadeaux.
Elle rapporte toujours la même chose. Par exemple, à moi, elle m'achète des vêtements.
À Guillaume, mon petit frère, elle rapporte des jouets ou des petites voitures.
Pour mon père, il y a toujours un livre ou un CD. Enfin, elle achète des chocolats à ses collègues.
Et pour Stéphanie, sa secrétaire, il y a toujours du parfum.

Exemple

1. *Madame Joubert leur téléphone tous les jours.* ☑
2. *Madame Joubert lui parle longtemps.* ☐
3. *Madame Joubert lui rapporte des cadeaux.* ☐
4. *Madame Joubert leur donne des vêtements.* ☐
5. *Madame Joubert leur donne des jouets.* ☐
6. *Madame Joubert lui donne des petites voitures.* ☐
7. *Madame Joubert leur donne des livres.* ☐
8. *Madame Joubert lui donne des CD.* ☐
9. *Madame Joubert lui donne des chocolats.* ☐
10. *Madame Joubert lui donne du parfum.* ☐

Name:

Order of object pronouns

- Normally, direct object pronouns and indirect object pronouns go before the verb:
  <u>direct object:</u> *Je **l'**ai vu aux Grandes Galeries.* – I saw **it** in the Grandes Galeries store.
  *Si tu **la** ranges bien, alors, d'accord.* – If you tidy **it** up well, then OK.
  <u>indirect object:</u> *Tu **m'**achètes ce robot?* – Would you buy **me** this robot?
- If you use a direct object pronoun (for instance, *le, la, les*) with one of the indirect object pronouns *me, te, nous* or *vous*, the indirect object pronoun comes first:
  *Si tu **<u>me</u> le** donnes, je vais ranger toute la maison.* – If you give **it <u>to me</u>**, I will tidy up the whole house.
  *Je vais **<u>te</u> l'**acheter.* – I will buy **it <u>for you</u>**.

- For each French sentence, tick the correct English translation.

1. *Mon stylo? D'accord, je te le prête.*
a) OK, I'll lend it to him. ☐
b) OK, I'll lend it to you. ☑ Exemple

2. *Tu as reçu une brochure du magasin? Tu me la lis?*
a) Would you read it to me? ☐
b) Would you read it to her? ☐

3. *Les documents? Oui, il nous les a montrés.*
a) Yes, we showed them to him. ☐
b) Yes, he showed them to us. ☐

4. *Vous voulez mes Nike? Non, je ne vous les vends pas.*
a) No, I'm not selling them to you. ☐
b) No, I'm not selling it to you. ☐

5. *Sophie a une tente pour trois personnes. Elle nous la propose.*
a) She's offering it to us. ☐
b) She's offering it to her. ☐

6. *Le paquet est urgent. Elle doit me l'envoyer vite.*
a) She must send me there quickly. ☐
b) She must send it to me quickly. ☐

7. *C'est une bonne vidéo. On te la recommande.*
a) We recommend it to you. ☐
b) We recommend you to her. ☐

8. *Quelle histoire extraordinaire! Qui vous l'a racontée?*
a) Who told it to you? ☐
b) Who told him about you? ☐

9. *Ces magazines? Arthur te les laisse pour le week-end.*
a) Arthur's leaving it for us over the weekend. ☐
b) Arthur's leaving them for you over the weekend. ☐

10. *Le nom de l'hôtel? Attendez, je vais vous le dire.*
a) Wait, I'll tell you about him. ☐
b) Wait, I'll give it to you. ☐

11. *Mon prof a beaucoup de questions. Il va me les poser demain.*
a) He will ask me them tomorrow. ☐
b) I will put them to him tomorrow. ☐

12. *La mère de Jack a une maison à la montagne. Mais est-ce qu'elle voudrait nous la louer?*
a) But would she rent it to us? ☐
b) But could we rent it to her? ☐

Name:

Disjunctive/emphatic pronouns 1

* *gronder* – to tell off

- You use a different set of personal pronouns when you want to put special emphasis on who does what.

	singular (one only)	**plural** (more than one)
1st person 2nd person 3rd person, masculine 3rd person, feminine	*moi* *toi* (to a friend or a young person) *lui* *elle*	*nous* *vous* (to a group of people, or to one unfamiliar adult) *eux* *elles*

- You use these pronouns after *c'est*: *C'est **toi**, Gabriel?* – Is that **you**, Gabriel?
  *C'est **lui**!* – It's **him**!
  for emphasis: ***Moi**? Non, Maman!* – **Me**? No, Mum!
  ***Toi**, tu es petit.* – **You** are small.
  after a comparative: *Tu es plus grand que **moi**.* – You are bigger than **me**.

- Ségolène is moaning about her life at school and her teachers.
  Read her letter and fill in the blanks with the correct pronoun.

Chère Becky

1. Exemple ......Moi......... *, je trouve les profs du collège très pénibles. Parce qu'ils sont plus vieux que* **2.** .... *, ils pense qu'ils savent tout. Mais* **3.** .... *, je pense que souvent, nous sommes plus intelligents qu'* **4.** .... *.*
En plus, **5.** .... *, on doit manger à la cantine, qui est dégoûtante.* **6.** .... *, ils ont une salle à manger spéciale. Mon copain Vincent,* **7.** .... *, il pense que ça n'a pas d'importance. Je ne suis pas d'accord.*
Les profs devraient avoir le même déjeuner que **8.** .... *. Et puis,* **9.** .... *, les élèves, on doit travailler dans de vieilles salles de classe. Mais les profs,* **10.** .... *, ils ont une belle salle des profs, juste repeinte.*
Et **11.** .... *, qu'est-ce que tu penses de ton collège?* **12.** .... *, tu as de meilleures notes que* **13.** .... *à l'école, alors tu n'as pas de problèmes avec les profs, peut-être!*

Amitiés

Ségolène

Name:

Disjunctive/emphatic pronouns 2

- You use a different set of personal pronouns when you want to put special emphasis on who does what. The same pronouns are also used after prepositions, for instance *à, de, pour, avec, sans, à côté de, sur, chez,* etc.

	singular (one only)	**plural** (more than one)
1st person 2nd person 3rd person, masculine 3rd person, feminine	*moi* *toi* (to a friend or a young person) *lui* *elle*	*nous* *vous* (to a group of people, or to one unfamiliar adult) *eux* *elles*

*Le poisson est **pour moi**.* – The fish is **for me**.
*La pizza est **pour toi**.* – The pizza is **for you**.
*Et **pour eux**?* – And **for them**?

***Pour elle**, la peau de banane.* – **For her**, the banana skin.
*Ici, je suis **chez moi**.* - This is **my place**, here.
*Retournez **chez vous**.* – Go back to **your place**.

- Read Céline's letter to her friend Katie and fill in the gaps with the right pronoun.

Chère Katie

Ce week-end, on va fêter l'anniversaire de ma copine Marion chez **1.** ......*elle* (Exemple)...... *. Malheureusement, Amir, l'ami de Marion, ne peut pas venir. Sans* **2.** .... *, c'est un peu triste. Les parents de Marion ont une grande maison. Chez* **3.** .... *, il y a un grand garage et même une piscine. Aujourd'hui, j'ai acheté deux CD.* Justified *est le cadeau pour Marion et* Crazy in love *est pour* **4.** .... *, parce que c'est mon groupe préféré.*

J'ai un nouveau petit ami qui s'appelle Simon. Bien sûr, je vais à la fête avec **5.** .... *. Nous allons tôt chez Marion samedi. Elle a besoin de* **6.** .... *pour préparer le garage, les boissons, la musique. On a aussi une surprise pour* **7.** ....*: des ballons pour décorer le garage.*

Pour **8.** .... *, les examens sont terminés, mais il y a des examens pour* **9.** .... *bientôt, je crois? Bon courage! Je pense à* **10.** .... *et je t'embrasse.*

Céline

P.-S. Voici une photo de Simon. Il est mignon, n'est-ce pas? Le garçon à côté de **11.** .... *, c'est David, son frère.*

Name:

Demonstrative pronouns

- The demonstrative pronoun *ce* is mainly used with *est* or *était* in the phrases *c'est* and *c'était*, which mean 'it is', 'this is', 'that is', 'it was', 'this was', 'that was'.
  ***C'est** une exposition de voitures.* – It's a car show.
- Note that *c'est* is used with a noun where in English, you use 'he' or 'she':
  ***C'est** un millionnaire.* – **He's** a millionaire.
- *Ça* is a demonstrative pronoun normally translated as 'it' or 'that'. It can refer to a general idea or to a particular thing.
  ***Ça** m'intéresse.* – That interests me.
  ***Ça**, c'est une Ferrari.* – That's a Ferrari.
- To point to something, you use the demonstrative pronouns *celui-ci* (this one), *celui-là* (that one).
- These demonstrative pronouns change according to the gender (masculine or feminine) and number (singular or plural) of the noun they replace.

	singular (one only)	**plural** (more than one)
masculine	*celui-ci, celui-là*	*ceux-ci, ceux-là*
feminine	*celle-ci, celle-là*	*celles-ci, celles-là*

Je voudrais celle-ci. – I would like this one. (= 'this car', *cette voiture*, feminine)

- For each sentence, underline what is being pointed to. For the gender of the nouns, check in the glossary at the bottom of the page.

Exemple

1. *Je voudrais celle-là.* — *le vélo – <u>la moto</u> – l'avion*
2. *Je voudrais ceux-ci.* — *les livres – le CD – le magazine*
3. *Je voudrais celles-là.* — *les canapés – la chaise – les tables*
4. *Je voudrais celle-ci.* — *le bracelet – la montre – les colliers*
5. *Je voudrais celui-ci.* — *le crayon – la lettre – les stylos*
6. *Je voudrais ça.* — *ma sœur – mon amie – mon ordinateur*
7. *Je voudrais ceux-là.* — *les carottes – les oranges – les haricots*
8. *Je voudrais celles-ci.* — *les baskets – le ballon – la casquette*
9. *Je voudrais celui-là.* — *les chapeaux – le casque – les lunettes*

l'avion **m** *la basket* *le canapé* *la carotte* *le chapeau*
le collier *le haricot* *le livre* *l'orange* **f** *le stylo* *la table*

Name:

Interrogative pronouns

- *Qui, qu'est-ce qui* and *qu'est-ce que* are interrogative pronouns.
- *Qui* translates as 'who': ***Qui*** *est là?* – **Who's** there?
- *Qu'est-ce qui* translates as 'what' and is used as the <u>subject</u> of the following verb (i.e. it refers to <u>what</u> does the action described by the verb): ***Qu'est-ce qui*** *se passe?* – **What's** happening?
- *Qu'est-ce que* (*qu'est-ce qu'* before a vowel) also translates as 'what', but is used as the <u>object</u> of the following verb: ***Qu'est-ce que*** *vous voulez?* – **What** do you want?

- The youth club is organising an open day (*journée portes ouvertes*). Here are some of the questions the club members have to answer first. Fill in the blanks with *qui, qu'est-ce qui* or *qu'est-ce que*.

1. Exemple: Qui .... *peut participer?*
2. Exemple: Qu'est-ce que .... *tu écris dans les lettres?*
3. Exemple: Qu'est-ce qui .... *est le moins cher, le jus d'orange ou le coca?*
4. .... *écrit les lettres?*
5. .... *prépare le site Web?*
6. .... *on écrit sur le site Web?*
7. .... *invites-tu à la journée portes ouvertes?*
8. .... *distribue les invitations?*
9. .... *apporte les boissons?*
10. .... *va attirer les visiteurs, de la musique, ou une vidéo?*
11. .... *nous mettons dans les sandwichs?*
12. .... *nous accrochons aux murs pour décorer?*
13. .... *nous montrons aux visiteurs?*
14. .... *va ranger la salle après?*

Name:

y and en

- *En* and *y* are pronouns.
- *En* replaces the noun when counting, or the preposition *de* + noun.
  *J'**en** ai six.* – I have got six (of them).
  *J'**en** ai peur.* – I'm afraid **of them**. (= of the children; *avoir peur de* – to be afraid of)
- *Y* replaces the prepositions *à*, or *dans*, or *sur* + noun. It can also mean 'there'.
  *Je n'**y** vais plus.* – I don't go **there** any more. (= in the neighbour's garden)

- Thomas is being quizzed by a prospective penfriend. Match the questions and the answers. Careful: there is one answer too many.

A
1. *Tu as des frères et sœurs?* — Exemple: C
2. *Tu visites quelquefois Paris?* ☐
3. *Tu assistes aux matchs de foot dans ta ville?* ☐
4. *Est-ce que tu aimes la viande?* ☐

a) *Non, je n'en mange jamais.*
b) *Oui, j'en bois le matin.*
c) *Oui, j'en ai deux.*
d) *Oui, j'y vais le samedi.*
e) *Oui, j'y vais tous les étés.*

B
1. *Tu as un examen cette année?* ☐
2. *Tu vas souvent à la piscine?* ☐
3. *Moi, je fais du rugby. Et toi?* ☐
4. *Tu as un correspondant étranger?* ☐

a) *J'y vais quelquefois l'été.*
b) *Oui, j'en fait dans ma chambre.*
c) *Non, je n'y joue pas.*
d) *Oui, j'en ai un en juin.*
e) *Oui, j'en ai un en Allemagne, Stefan.*

C
1. *Tu aimes la musique?* ☐
2. *Tu fais du piano?* ☐
3. *Il y a des concerts dans ton collège?* ☐
4. *Tu aimes ton collège?* ☐

a) *Oui, et j'y participe souvent.*
b) *Oui, j'en veux bien.*
c) *Oui, je m'y intéresse beaucoup.*
d) *Non, je n'en suis pas très content. Il est trop grand.*
e) *Non, je n'en joue pas.*

Name:

être

* *très serrés* – tightly packed

- Note the personal pronouns in the cartoon: *Il* can mean 'he' or 'it': ***Il** est midi.* – **It** is midday.
- *On* is used to talk about people in general: ***On** est très serrés.* – **We** are tightly packed.
- *Ils* is used for a mix of men and women (or masculine and feminine nouns), *elles* for women (or feminine nouns) only:
  ***Ils** sont sympa.* – **They** are nice. (talking about all the Zylbeks)
  ***Elles** sont sympa.* – **They** are nice. (talking about the two women, Séverine and Saïda)
- Here is the present tense of the verb *être*:

je suis	*nous sommes*
tu es	*vous êtes*
il/elle/on est	*ils/elles sont*

- *Être* is an important verb. It can mean 'to be':
  ***Je suis** le chef des Zylbeks.* – **I am** the chief of the Zylbeks.
- It is also used to form the perfect tense of some verbs: *Je suis allé(e), Vous êtes parti(e)(s)*

- A local journalist is interviewing holiday-makers on the French Riviera.
  Fill in the blanks with the correct form of the verb *être*.

- *Aujourd'hui, je* **1.** ....Exemple: suis.... *sur la côte d'Azur et j'interviewe des touristes.*
- *Madame, vous* **2.** .... *à l'hôtel ou dans un camping?*
- *Mon mari et moi, on* **3.** .... *à l'hôtel. Mais ma fille et ses amies* **4.** .... *dans un camping.*
- *Vous* **5.** .... *contents de votre hôtel?*
- *Oui, il* **6.** .... *confortable, mais les chambres* **7.** .... *trop petites. Et puis, nous* **8.** .... *loin de la plage.*
- *Quel âge as-tu?*
- *J'ai 15 ans.*
- *Tu* **9.** .... *dans un hôtel ou dans un camping?*
- *Je* **10.** .... *dans un camping avec mes amies.*
- *Où* **11.** .... *tes amies?*
- *Elles* **12.** .... *dans le magasin là-bas.*
- *Est-ce qu'il* **13.** .... *confortable, votre camping?*
- *Notre tente, oui. Elle* **14.** .... *confortable. Mais les douches du camping* **15.** .... *un peu sales.*

Name:

avoir

* *l'infirmerie* – sickroom
* *la récréation* – break

3

- Here is the present tense of the verb *avoir*:

j'ai	*nous avons*
tu as	*vous avez*
il/elle/on a	*ils/elles ont*
il y a	

- *Avoir* is an important verb. It can mean 'to have (got)':
  ***Nous avons** maths.* – **We've got** maths.
- It is also part of many set phrases:
  ***Il y a** un problème.* – **There is** a problem. ***Il y a** des nuages.* – **There are** clouds.
  C'est l'anniversaire d'Arnaud. ***Il a** 15 ans.* – It's Arnaud's birthday. **He is** 15 (years old). ***J'ai** froid.* – **I'm** cold.
- It is also used to form the perfect tense of many verbs.
  ***J'ai mangé** une pomme.* – **I ate** an apple.

- Simon is on holiday at the seaside. The tourist office is conducting a survey and asks him a few questions. Fill in the blanks with the correct form of the verb *avoir* (including *il y a*).

Exemple

- *Tu* **1.** ....as........ *des frères et sœurs?*
- *J'* **2.** .... *un frère et une sœur, qui s'appellent Erwan et Noémie.*
- *Quel âge* **3.** .... *-ils?*
- *Erwan* **4.** .... *16 ans et Noémie* **5.** .... *14 ans.*
- *Où passes-tu tes vacances?*
- *Nous* **6.** .... *une cousine, Sophie. Elle* **7.** .... *15 ans. Les parents de Sophie* **8.** .... *une petite maison au bord de la mer. Il y* **9.** .... *quatre chambres dans la maison, c'est pratique.*
- *Tu* **10.** .... *des activités préférées?*
- *À la plage, il y* **11.** .... *un club de voile. En ville, il y* **12.** .... *des cafés et des cinémas.*
- *Vous* **13.** .... *une voiture?*
- *Non, nous* **14.** .... *moins de18 ans! Mais Noémie, Sophie et moi, on* **15.** .... *des vélos. Moi, j'* **16.** .... *un VTT, mais pas Noémie et Sophie. Elles* **17.** .... *des vélos ordinaires. Erwan* **18.** .... *16 ans, alors il* **19.** .... *une petite moto.*

Name:

Present tense of –er verbs 1

- Here is the present tense of *aimer* (to like, to love), a regular *–er* verb (singular forms only):
  *j'aim**e***
  *tu aim**es***
  *il/elle/on aim**e***
- The form *aimer* is called the infinitive of the verb. You simply remove the ending *–er* from the infinitive. You are left with the stem (*aim-*) and you add the present tense endings (in **bold** in the list above) to the stem.
  ***J'aime** cette robe.* – **I like** this dress.
- Some regular *–er* verbs show a small difference in the pattern:
  In *acheter* (to buy) and *préférer* (to prefer), the *e*, or last *é*, in the stem changes to *è*.
  *j'ach**è**te* / *je préf**è**re*
  *tu ach**è**tes* / *tu préf**è**res*
  *il/elle/on ach**è**te* / *il/elle/on préf**è**re*
  In verbs ending in *–yer* like *essayer* (to try, to try on), or *payer* (to pay), the *y* in the stem usually becomes an *i*:
  *j'essa**ie***
  *tu essa**ies***
  *il/elle/on essa**ie***

- Read the English sentences. In parts A and B, match the half sentences in French to make up a correct translation by drawing a line and adding a number. Careful: there is one half sentence too many. Then, in part C, translate the sentences into French.

A
1. She's buying a jacket.
2. I prefer black shoes.
3. Are you trying on the blue trousers?
4. Do you like the red jumper?

Tu essaies	*les chaussures noires.*
Exemple 1. *Elle achète*	*le pull rouge?*
Elle préfère	*le pantalon bleu?*
Je préfère	*une veste.*
Tu aimes	

B
1. She prefers boots in winter.
2. I am paying with my card.
3. We often eat at the cafeteria.
4. He is wearing a funny shirt.

Il porte	*avec ma carte.*
Elle préfère	*les bottes en hiver.*
Elle porte	*une chemise amusante.*
On mange	*souvent à la cafétéria.*
Je paie	

C
1. You try on the black jacket. ....
2. She is paying with her card. ....
3. He works in the cafeteria. ....
4. Do you buy your shoes here? ....

Name:

Present tense of –er verbs 2

* *le charbon* – coal

3

- Here is the present tense of *aimer*, a regular *–er* verb (plural forms only):

  *nous aim**ons***
  *vous aim**ez***
  *ils/elles aim**ent***

- The form *aimer* is called the infinitive of the verb. You simply remove the ending *–er* from the infinitive. You are left with the stem (*aim-*) and you add the present tense endings (in **bold** in the list above) to the stem.
  ***Vous aimez** votre travail?* – **Do you like** your job?
- Some regular *–er* verbs show a small difference in the pattern: In *acheter* (to buy) and *préférer* (to prefer), the *e*, or last *é*, in the stem changes to *è* with *ils* or *elles*.

nous achetons	*nous préferons*
vous achetez	*vous préferez*
ils/elles achètent	*ils/elles préfèrent*

  The *nous* ending for *manger* (to eat), *nager* (to swim) and other verbs ending in *–ger* is *–**e**ons*.

  nous mangeons
  vous mangez
  ils/elles mangent

  The *nous* ending for *commencer* (to start, to begin) and other verbs ending in *–cer* is *–**ç**ons*.

  nous commençons
  vous commencez
  ils/elles commencent

- All the French sentences below contain a mistake. Cross out the mistake, choose a verb from the list at the bottom and write the correct verb form in the space provided.

1.	They are buying a motorbike.	*Elles ~~mangent~~ une moto.*	Exemple: achètent
2.	We are working at the service station.	*Nous jouons à la station-service.*	....
3.	Do you prefer to leave?	*Vous marchez partir?*	....
4.	We start the meeting at 4pm.	*Nous marchons la réunion à 16 heures.*	....
5.	We are swimming for the regional team.	*Nous fermons pour l'équipe régionale.*	....
6.	They are preparing a meeting.	*Elles décident une réunion.*	....
7.	The factories often close.	*Les usines montent souvent.*	....
8.	We eat in the works' canteen.	*Nous chantons à la cantine de l'entreprise.*	....
9.	You are buying too much furniture.	*Vous préférez trop de meubles.*	....
10.	We buy our tickets at the ticket office.	*Nous préparons nos billets au guichet.*	....
11.	The directors decide to close the office.	*Les directeurs lavent de fermer le bureau.*	....
12.	First, you wash the cars.	*D'abord, vous fermez les voitures.*	....

acheter *commencer* *décider* *fermer* *laver* *manger* *nager* *préférer* *préparer* *travailler*

Name:

Present tense of –ir verbs

* *le ver de terre* – earthworm
* *la poêle* – frying pan

- Here is the present tense of *choisir* (to choose), a regular *–ir* verb:

*je chois**is***	*nous chois**issons***
*tu chois**is***	*vous chois**issez***
*il/elle/on chois**it***	*ils/elles chois**issent***

- The form *choisir* is called the infinitive of the verb. You simply remove the ending *–ir* from the infinitive.

  You are left with the stem (*chois-*) and you add the present tense endings (in **bold** in the list above) to the stem.
  ***On choisit** des pommes de terre.* – **We choose** potatoes.

- The most useful regular *–ir* verbs apart from *choisir* are *finir* (to finish, to end), *remplir* (to fill up, to fill in) and *vomir* (to be sick).
  Be careful: many verbs ending in *–ir* are **NOT** regular.

- Fill in the gaps with the correct form of *choisir*, *finir* or *remplir*.

1. *Tu* ......Exemple choisis...... *la glace au chocolat ou la glace à la fraise?*
2. *Elles* .... *leurs devoirs avant de regarder la télé.*
3. *Nous* .... *les blancs sur la feuille de travail.*
4. *Je* .... *ma valise de pulls: il fait froid à la montagne!*
5. *L'école* .... *le 21 juillet cette année.*
6. *Pour mes examens, je* .... *maths, physique et anglais.*
7. *Tu* .... *ce vase d'eau, s'il te plaît?*
8. *Le film* .... *trop tard pour moi.*
9. *Pour louer une voiture, vous* .... *d'abord cette feuille.*
10. *Je* .... *mon petit déjeuner et j'arrive!*
11. *Les garçons* .... *souvent le VTT.*
12. *Tu* .... *ton travail à quelle heure?*

Name:

Present tense of –re verbs

- Here is the present tense of *vendre* (to sell), a regular *–re* verb.

*je vend**s***	*nous vend**ons***
*tu vend**s***	*vous vend**ez***
il/elle/on vend	*ils/elles vend**ent***

- The form *vendre* is called the infinitive of the verb. You simply remove the ending *–re* from the infinitive. You are left with the stem (*vend-*) and you add the present tense endings (in **bold** in the list above) to the stem.
***Il vend** sa voiture.* – **He is selling** his car.
- Here are a few other common regular *–re* verbs: *attendre* (to wait), *descendre* (to go down), *entendre* (to hear), *perdre* (to lose), *rendre* (to give back), *répondre* (to answer).
Be careful: many verbs ending in *–re* are **NOT** regular.

- Change each singular sentence to its plural form, and each plural sentence to its singular form.

1. *Tu rends le livre à la bibiothèque?* Exemple: Vous rendez le livre à la bibliothèque?
2. *Elles vendent des glaces sur la plage.* Exemple: Elle vend des glaces sur la plage.
3. *Nous descendons à la prochaine station.* ....
4. *Tu réponds aux questions du prof?* ....
5. *Nous perdons souvent de l'argent.* ....
6. *Vous entendez la musique à la radio?* ....
7. *Je réponds au téléphone.* ....
8. *Il entend un bruit dans le moteur.* ....
9. *J'attends les vacances avec impatience.* ....
10. *Vous vendez aussi des vêtements?* ....
11. *Elle attend le train de 10 heures 17.* ....
12. *Ils descendent à la cave.* ....

Name:

Present tense of reflexive verbs 1

- Reflexive verbs have two sets of personal pronouns.
  On se *brosse les dents.* – **We** brush our teeth.
- Here are the singular forms of *se baigner* (to have a swim): ***je me*** *baigne*, ***tu te*** *baignes*, ***il/elle/on se*** *baigne*
- Note *se lever* (to get up) and *s'appeler* (to be called): these reflexive verbs are regular *–er* verbs, but they have a small irregularity, shown here in bold.

*je me l**è**ve*	*je m'appe**ll**e*
*tu te l**è**ves*	*tu t'appe**ll**es*
*il/elle/on se l**è**ve*	*il/elle/on s'appe**ll**e*

Tu t'appelles *Lecroc, c'est ça?* – **Your name's** Lecroc, is that right?
On se lève *tard.* – **We get up** late.

- Amir has made a friend while on holiday in Tunisia. This is their conversation. The words in the French sentences are jumbled up. Put them in the right order.

1. *appelles Karim, père tu comme t' mon*
   Your name is Karim, like my father. **Exemple** Tu t'appelles Karim, comme mon père.
2. *dans se le il repose hamac*
   He is having a rest in the hammock. ....
3. *se vers heures il 4 réveille*
   He wakes up around 4pm. ....
4. *vacances, je bien pendant amuse les m'*
   During the holidays, I have fun. ....
5. *dans me Méditerranée je la baigne*
   I swim in the Mediterranean. ....
6. *lève les se jours à on tous midi*
   We get up every day at midday. ....
7. *rues dans me les promène vieilles je*
   I walk around in the old streets. ....
8. *aux intéresses t' bateaux? tu*
   Are you interested in boats? ....
9. *intéresse m' la non, pêche je à*
   No, I'm interested in fishing. ....
10. *te ta tu avec disputes sœur?*
    Do you fight with your sister? ....
11. *bien je avec m' elle non, entends*
    No, I get on well with her. ....
12. *les à jours elle minuit couche tous se*
    She goes to bed at midnight every day. ....

Name:

Present tense of reflexive verbs 2

* <u>Reflexive</u> verbs have two sets of personal pronouns.
  Nous nous voyons *dans la rue.* – **We see each other** in the street.
  Vous vous rencontrez *à l'église.* – **You meet** at the church.
  Ils se retrouvent *dans le jardin.* – **They meet up** in the garden.
* Here are the plural forms of *se voir* (to see each other), which is also an irregular verb.
  nous nous *voyons*
  vous vous *voyez*
  ils/elles se *voient*
* Note *se lever* (to get up) and *s'appeler* (to be called; to call each other): these reflexive verbs are regular *–er* verbs, but they have a small irregularity, shown here in **bold**.

nous nous levons	*nous nous appelons*
vous vous levez	*vous vous appelez*
*ils/elles se l**è**vent*	*ils/elles s'appe**ll**ent*

* *Tournez!* – Action!

3

* Alexandre answers questions on his relationship with his girlfriend Astrid. Write the correct form of the verb in the blank.

- *Ma copine s'appelle Astrid. Elle habite dans une autre ville, mais nous (s'écrire)* **1.** Exemple: nous écrivons *tous les jours.*
- *Et vous (se voir)* **2.** .... *le week-end, n'est-ce pas?*
- *Oui. En général, nous (se retrouver)* **3.** .... *au cinéma, ou au club de jeunes.*
  Malheureusement, ses parents (se disputer) **4.** .... *souvent. Ensuite, ils (s'appeler)* **5.** .... *au téléphone. Mais l'atmosphère n'est pas sympa, alors, on ne va pas chez elle.*
- *Et vous (s'intéresser)* **6.** .... *au sport?*
- *Pas beaucoup. L'été, nous allons à la plage et nous (se baigner)* **7.** .... *Ou bien nous (se promener)* **8.** .... *dans les dunes. Ce n'est pas vraiment du sport.*
  J'ai des amis qui (s'intéresser) **9.** .... *beaucoup aux bateaux. Mais pas nous.*
- *Vous (se disputer)* **10.** .... *quelquefois?*
- *Non! Pas vraiment.*
- *Donc, vous (s'entendre)* **11.** .... *bien, Astrid et toi?*
- *Oui, et nous (s'amuser)* **12.** .... *bien ensemble.*

Name:

Modal verbs

- *Vouloir* (to want), *devoir* (must, to have to), *pouvoir* (can, to be able to) are three important verbs.
  Je veux *devenir astronaute.* – **I want** to become an astronaut.
  Vous devez *étudier la physique.* – **You must** study physics.
  Est-ce que ***vous pouvez*** *me conseiller?* – **Can you** advise me?
- All three verbs are irregular.

vouloir:	***devoir:***	***pouvoir:***
je veux	*je dois*	*je peux*
tu veux	*tu dois*	*tu peux*
il/elle/on veut	*il/elle/on doit*	*il/elle/on peut*
nous voulons	*nous devons*	*nous pouvons*
vous voulez	*vous devez*	*vous pouvez*
ils/elles veulent	*ils/elles doivent*	*ils/elles peuvent*

- Read the short dialogues and complete them with a form of *vouloir, devoir* or *pouvoir*.

1. boy: *Je* Exemple veux *sortir ce soir, Papa!*
father: *Non, c'est impossible. Tu ne* .... *pas sortir ce soir, tu as des devoirs.*
2. man: *Est-ce que vous* .... *réparer mon vélo?*
bicycle shop assistant: *Oui, c'est possible. Je* .... *le réparer pour mardi, par exemple.*
3. woman 1: *Vous* .... *encore un morceau de gâteau?*
woman 2: *Non, merci. Je* .... *partir. J'ai un train dans dix minutes.*
4. woman: *Je* .... *un nouveau passeport.*
office worker: *D'abord, vous* .... *remplir cette feuille, Madame: nom, prénom, adresse, ...*
5. pupil 1: *Le prof de maths* .... *me voir après le cours.*
pupil 2: *Bon courage!*
6. boy: *À 18 ans, on* .... *conduire une voiture.*
girl: *Oui, mais on* .... *avoir son permis de conduire.*
7. girl: *Je* .... *partir en vacances avec mes copines, mais mes parents ne le* .... *pas. Ce n'est pas juste!*
8. boy, 14: *Je* .... *une moto pour mon anniversaire.*
mother: *Mais ce n'est pas possible! On* .... *avoir 16 ans pour rouler en moto.*
9. girl: *Mes parents* .... *partir en vacances en octobre, cette année. Ils préfèrent les vacances en automne.*
boy: *Ah bon? Mes parents ne* .... *pas partir, cette année. Ils n'ont pas d'argent.*
10. boy: *Est-ce que les élèves* .... *rester au collège jusqu'à 16 ans?*
girl: *Oui, c'est obligatoire. Ensuite, ils* .... *aller au lycée, ou trouver un travail.*

Name:

Present tense of aller, venir, savoir

- *Aller* (to go), *venir* (to come) and *savoir* (to know something, to know how to, can) are three important verbs.
  *Si **je vais** à la fête de Marie avec toi ...* – If **I go** to Marie's party with you ...
  *... **tu viens** chez le dentiste avec moi.* – ... **you're coming** to the dentist with me.
  *Tous tes amis **vont** chez Marie, **tu sais**.* – All your friends **are going** to Marie's, **you know**.
  ***Il sait** chanter.* – **He can** sing.
- All three verbs are irregular.

aller:	***venir:***	***savoir:***
je vais	*je viens*	*je sais*
tu vas	*tu viens*	*tu sais*
il/elle/on va	*il/elle/on vient*	*il/elle/on sait*
nous allons	*nous venons*	*nous savons*
vous allez	*vous venez*	*vous savez*
ils/elles vont	*ils/elles viennent*	*ils/elles savent*

- You sometimes need *aller* to talk about future events.
  Je vais partir en vacances. – I'm going to go on holiday.
- *Revenir* (to come back) and *devenir* (to become) follow the same pattern as *venir*.

- For each situation, read the French sentences. Fill in the blanks with the correct form of *aller*, *venir* (*devenir*, *revenir*) or *savoir*. Then match them with the correct translation. Careful: for each situation, there is one translation too many.

A
1. *Nous* ...Exemple: allons... *à la plage.* [Exemple: d]
2. *Sophie et Dorothée* .... *avec nous.* [ ]
3. *Elles* .... *faire du ski nautique.* [ ]

a) They know how to do water skiing. **c)** They're going swimming.
b) Sophie and Dorothée are coming with us. **d)** We're going to the beach.

B
1. *On* .... *en vacances en février.* [ ]
2. *Je* .... *faire du bobsleigh.* [ ]
3. *On* .... *tout bronzés.* [ ]

a) We come back all tanned. **c)** I know how to do bobsleighing.
b) We're going on holiday in February. **d)** They're going to go bobsleighing.

C
1. *Je* .... *à Rome avec mon ami.* [ ]
2. *Il* .... *parler italien.* [ ]
3. *Nous* .... *le 3 juin.* [ ]

a) We're coming back on June 3rd. **c)** I'm going to Rome with my friend.
b) He can speak Italian. **d)** He's coming back on June 3rd.

D
1. *Mon frère, Étienne,* .... *très bien jouer au foot.* [ ]
2. *Cette semaine, il* .... *capitaine de l'équipe junior.* [ ]
3. *Il* .... *au stade le mercredi et le samedi.* [ ]

a) This week, he becomes captain of the junior team. **c)** He goes to the stadium on Wednesdays and Saturdays.
b) He goes to play football every week. **d)** My brother, Étienne, can play football very well.

Name:

Present tense of prendre (apprendre, comprendre)

- *Prendre* (to take), *apprendre* (to learn) and *comprendre* (to understand) are irregular verbs and all follow the same pattern.
  ***On apprend** à faire des photos.* – **We learn** to take photos.
  ***Vous prenez** l'appareil.* – **You take** the camera.
  ***Nous comprenons**.* – **We understand**.
- Here is the present tense:

	je prends	*nous prenons*
	tu prends	*vous prenez*
	il/elle/on prend	*ils/elles prennent*

- Fill in the blank with the correct form of *prendre*, *apprendre* or *comprendre*.

1. They understand the questions. – *Elles* ..... Exemple comprennent ..... *les questions.*
2. Do you have tea at breakfast? – *Tu* .... *du thé au petit déjeuner?*
3. I understand algebra, but not physics. – *Je* .... *l'algèbre, mais pas la physique.*
4. Chang understands Chinese, but he can't speak it. – *Chang* .... *le chinois, mais il ne le parle pas.*
5. My parents take three sugars in their coffee. – *Mes parents* .... *trois sucres dans leur café.*
6. We understand Arabic a little. – *Nous* .... *un peu l'arabe.*
7. I am learning German. – *J'* .... *l'allemand.*
8. Caroline is learning the piano. – *Caroline* .... *le piano.*
9. To get to New York you fly. – *Pour aller à New York on* .... *l'avion.*
10. They take the train because it's comfortable. – *Ils* .... *le train parce que c'est confortable.*
11. Are you learning to drive? – *Vous* .... *à conduire?*
12. We learn Spanish at 12. – *On* .... *l'espagnol à 12 ans.*

Name:

Present tense of sortir (partir), courir

- *Courir* (to run) and *partir* (to go away, to leave) are two irregular verbs. They follow slightly different patterns. *Sortir* (to go out) follows the same pattern as *partir*.
  ***On part** ce soir.* – **We're leaving** tonight.
  ***Vous sortez** par ici.* – **You're going out** this way.
  *Et si les gardiens **courent** aussi?* – What if the wardens **run** too?

partir:	***courir:***
je pars	*je cours*
tu pars	*tu cours*
il/elle/on part	*il/elle/on court*
nous partons	*nous courons*
vous partez	*vous courez*
ils/elles partent	*ils/elles courent*

- Every year, Samuel and his friend Stéphane take part in an annual sporting event for runners and cyclists. Fill in the blanks with the correct form of the verb.

On (partir) **1.** ......Exemple: part...... *tôt le matin. Les cyclistes (partir)* **2.** .... *les premiers, à 6 heures. Les coureurs à pied (partir)* **3.** .... *ensuite à 6 heures 30. On (sortir)* **4.** .... *de la ville. Les cyclistes (courir)* **5.** .... *pendant 50 kilomètres. Les coureurs à pied (courir)* **6.** .... *pendant 20 kilomètres. Mon ami Stéphane et moi, nous (partir)* **7.** .... *à pied ensemble. Mais Stéphane (courir)* **8.** .... *plus vite que moi et je reste seul. Pendant les 10 premiers kilomètres, je (courir)* **9.** .... *vite. Les gens (sortir)* **10.** .... *de leur maison pour regarder. Ils disent «Tu (courir)* **11.** .... *bien! Bravo!» C'est sympa. À la fin, tout le monde (courir)* **12.** .... *lentement. On voit même des coureurs à pied qui ne (courir)* **13.** .... *plus, qui marchent. Quand on arrive, on est très fatigués, mais contents. Le soir, on ne (sortir)* **14.** .... *pas, on rentre dormir.*

Name:

Present tense of faire and lire

- *Faire* (to do, to make) is an important verb and it follows an irregular pattern. *Lire* (to read) is also irregular, and follows a pattern of its own.
  Je fais *mes devoirs.* – **I'm doing** my homework.
  Lucas ***lit*** *un magazine.* – Lucas **is reading** a magazine.
  Ils font *leurs devoirs.* – **They're doing** their homework.
  Ils lisent *des magazines.* – **They're reading** magazines.

faire:	***lire:***
je fais	*je lis*
tu fais	*tu lis*
il/elle/on fait	*il/elle/on lit*
nous faisons	*nous lisons*
vous faites	*vous lisez*
ils/elles font	*ils/elles lisent*

- Make up 12 sentences, choosing one phrase from each column and writing the correct form of the verb. Then translate your sentences into English.

Exemple On fait du foot. — **Exemple** We play football.

je	*lire un magazine*
tu	*faire la vaisselle*
il	*faire de la musique*
Aurélien	*faire du piano*
elle	*faire du foot*
Émilie	*lire une lettre*
on	*faire de la planche à roulettes*
nous	*faire les magasins*
vous	*faire de l'équitation*
ils	*lire un livre*
mes parents	*faire un devoir de maths*
elles	*faire la cuisine*

Present tense of dire, (d)écrire, recevoir

KESTUDI? = Qu'est-ce que tu dis?

* *le texto* – text message

- *Dire* (to say, to tell), *écrire* (to write) and *recevoir* (to get, to receive) are three irregular verbs. They all follow different patterns.

dire:	**écrire:**	**recevoir:**
je dis	*j'écris*	*je reçois*
tu dis	*tu écris*	*tu reçois*
il/elle/on dit	*il/elle/on écrit*	*il/elle/on reçoit*
nous disons	*nous écrivons*	*nous recevons*
vous dites	*vous écrivez*	*vous recevez*
ils/elles disent	*ils/elles écrivent*	*ils/elles reçoivent*

*Les sondages **disent**…* – The surveys **say**…
*Les jeunes **écrivent** beaucoup de mails.* – Young people **write** many e-mails.
***Ils reçoivent** aussi beaucoup de texto.* – **They** also **get** many text messages.

- *Décrire* (to describe) follows the same pattern as *écrire*.

- A journalist interviews Madame Lacoste, who works for the council, at the Good Neighbours office. Fill in the blank with the correct form of *dire, écrire, décrire* or *recevoir*.

Madame Lacoste (décrire) **1.** Exemple: décrit .... *son travail*

- *Vous me (dire)* **2.** .... *ce que vous faites, Madame Lacoste?*
- *Nous (recevoir)* **3.** .... *beaucoup de lettres ici. Dans mon bureau, je (recevoir)* **4.** .... *100 lettres par jour.*
- *Que (dire)* **5.** .... *les lettres?*
- *Les gens (écrire)* **6.** .... *parce qu'ils ont des problèmes. Par exemple, cette dame (écrire)* **7.** .... *parce que le chien de son voisin fait trop de bruit. Cet homme (dire)* **8.** .... *qu'il est dans un fauteuil roulant, mais il n'y a pas d'ascenseur dans son immeuble. Il (décrire)* **9.** .... *ses problèmes en détail. C'est une vie difficile.*
- *Est-ce que vous (recevoir)* **10.** .... *aussi des mails?*
- *Des mails, oui. Nous (recevoir)* **11.** .... *aussi des texto, mais rarement.*
- *Quels conseils donnez-vous?*
- *Nous (dire)* **12.** .... *aux gens de rester calmes, de parler à leurs voisins.*
- *Vous (écrire)* **13.** .... *toutes les réponses vous-même, Madame Lacoste?*
- *Non. J' (écrire)* **14.** .... *20 réponses, par jour moi-même. Pour le reste, j'ai deux secrétaires.*

Name:

Present tense of ouvrir, mettre, boire

- *Ouvrir* (to open), *mettre* (to put) and *boire* (to drink) are three irregular verbs. They all follow different patterns.

ouvrir:	***mettre:***	***boire:***
j'ouvre	*je mets*	*je bois*
tu ouvres	*tu mets*	*tu bois*
il/elle/on ouvre	*il/elle/on met*	*il/elle/on boit*
nous ouvrons	*nous mettons*	*nous buvons*
vous ouvrez	*vous mettez*	*vous buvez*
ils/elles ouvrent	*ils/elles mettent*	*ils/elles boivent*

3

* *la dinde* – turkey
* *le four* – oven
* *mettre le couvert* – to set the table
* *les invités* – guests

- It's Christmas time, and the chores as well as the pleasures have to be shared. On the back of this sheet make sentences for each phrase (**1**–**8**):
  a) describing what one person does, then
  b) what several people do,
  c) giving instructions to one person, then
  d) to several people.
  So for each phrase, you will be making four sentences.

1. *mettre les décorations sur le sapin de Noël*

a) Exemple Il/Mon père met les décorations sur le sapin de Noël.

b) Exemple Elles/Ma mère et ma sœur mettent les décorations sur le sapin de Noël.

c) Exemple Tu mets les décorations sur le sapin de Noël.

d) Exemple Vous mettez les décorations sur le sapin de Noël.

2. *mettre la dinde* au four**

3. *mettre le couvert**

4. *ouvrir les bouteilles*

5. *ouvrir la porte aux invités**

6. *ouvrir les cadeaux*

7. *boire du vin*

8. *boire du champagne*

Name:

Present tense of connaître, vivre, voir

Vous connaissez *La Désirade? C'est une petite île des Caraïbes. Les habitants* ***vivent*** *dans des villages au bord de la mer. Quand on se baigne,* ***on voit*** *des poissons exotiques. Moi,* ***je vis*** *dans un bungalow près de la plage. De la plage,* ***je vois*** *la Guadeloupe.* ***Je connais*** *la Guadeloupe et la Martinique, mais* ***je*** *ne* ***connais*** *pas la France. C'est trop loin.*

- *Connaître* (to know – a place or a person), *vivre* (to live) and *voir* (to see) are three irregular verbs. They all follow different patterns.

connaître:	***vivre:***	***voir:***
je connais	*je vis*	*je vois*
tu connais	*tu vis*	*tu vois*
il/elle/on connaît	*il/elle/on vit*	*il/elle/on voit*
nous connaissons	*nous vivons*	*nous voyons*
vous connaissez	*vous vivez*	*vous voyez*
ils/elles connaissent	*ils/elles vivent*	*ils/elles voient*

- Use a phrase from each column to translate the English sentences. Use the correct form of the verb.

Je	*connaître*	*à côté de la rivière.*
Je	*vivre*	*dans une petite maison.*
Tu	*voir*	*des coquillages rares.*
Elle		*la mer.*
Nous		*le musée, n'est-ce pas?*
Vous		*les bateaux tous les matins.*
Vous		*les montagnes.*
Ils		*les voisins.*
Du haut de la tour, on		*tout le monde.*
Le vieil homme		*toutes les plantes.*
Les flamants		*très près de la plage.*
Les vieux habitants du village		*seul.*

1. We live in a small house. **Exemple** Nous vivons dans une petite maison.
2. I know the neighbours. ....
3. They see the mountains. ....
4. From the top of the tower, you see the sea. ....
5. You know the museum, don't you? ....
6. You live very close to the beach. ....
7. The flamingoes live by the river. ....
8. I see the boats every morning. ....
9. The old villagers know everyone. ....
10. She knows all the plants. ....
11. You see rare seashells. ....
12. The old man lives alone. ....

Name:

Negative forms

- To say that something does **NOT** happen, you put the verb in the negative. You use *ne…pas* either side of the verb: *Je **ne** vole **pas**.* – I do**n't** steal.
- There are other types of negative phrases, for instance:
  *Je **ne** connais **personne** (qui vole).* – I do**n't** know **anybody** (who steals).
  *Je **ne** vole **plus**.* – I do**n't** steal **any more**. *Je **ne** vole **jamais**.* – I **never** steal. *Je **ne** vole **rien**.* – I do**n't** steal **anything**.
  *Je **ne** vole **aucun** bijou.* – I do**n't** steal **any** jewel. *Je **ne** vole **pas grand-chose**.* – I do**n't** steal **much**.
- Some of these phrases can be used at the start of a sentence:
  ***Personne ne** vole.* – **Nobody** steals. ***Rien ne** disparaît.* – **Nothing** disappears.

* *le bijou* – jewel

- Which French sentence is the best match for the English sentence?

1. The class won't do their maths homework.
- **a)** *Le devoir de maths? Je ne fais jamais mes devoirs!* ☐
- **b)** *Je ne fais pas mon devoir de maths.* ☐
- **c)** *Personne ne fait le devoir de maths.* Exemple ☑

2. There aren't many attractions on the beach.
- **a)** *Nous ne faisons rien à la plage.* ☐
- **b)** *Il n'y a pas grand-chose à faire à la plage.* ☐
- **c)** *Il n'y a personne à la plage.* ☐

3. People in the village are not Marine's friends.
- **a)** *Marine n'a aucun ami dans le village.* ☐
- **b)** *Il n'y a rien dans le village pour les amis de Marine.* ☐
- **c)** *Les amis de Marine n'habitent pas dans le village.* ☐

4. Fish have stopped feeding here.
- **a)** *Les poissons n'ont rien à manger.* ☐
- **b)** *Les poissons ne mangent plus ici.* ☐
- **c)** *On ne mange jamais de poisson.* ☐

5. Grown-ups don't want to go to the youth club.
- **a)** *Les jeunes ne veulent aucun adulte au club.* ☐
- **b)** *Il n'y a pas grand-chose pour les jeunes au club.* ☐
- **c)** *Les adultes ne vont jamais au club de jeunes.* ☐

6. Cyclists used to go to the town centre, but don't now.
- **a)** *Les cyclistes ne vont plus dans le centre-ville.* ☐
- **b)** *Il n'y a aucun cycliste dans le centre-ville.* ☐
- **c)** *Les cyclistes ne font rien dans le centre-ville.* ☐

7. There isn't much for tourists to do in Saint-Gilles.
- **a)** *Il n'y a jamais de touristes à Saint-Gilles.* ☐
- **b)** *Il n'y a rien pour les touristes à Saint-Gilles.* ☐
- **c)** *Il n'y a plus de touristes à Saint-Gilles.* ☐

8. In the spring, people don't swim in the Loire river.
- **a)** *Personne ne se baigne dans la Loire.* ☐
- **b)** *Les enfants ne se baignent pas dans la Loire.* ☐
- **c)** *On ne se baigne pas dans la Loire au printemps.* ☐

Name:

Negative forms with reflexive verbs

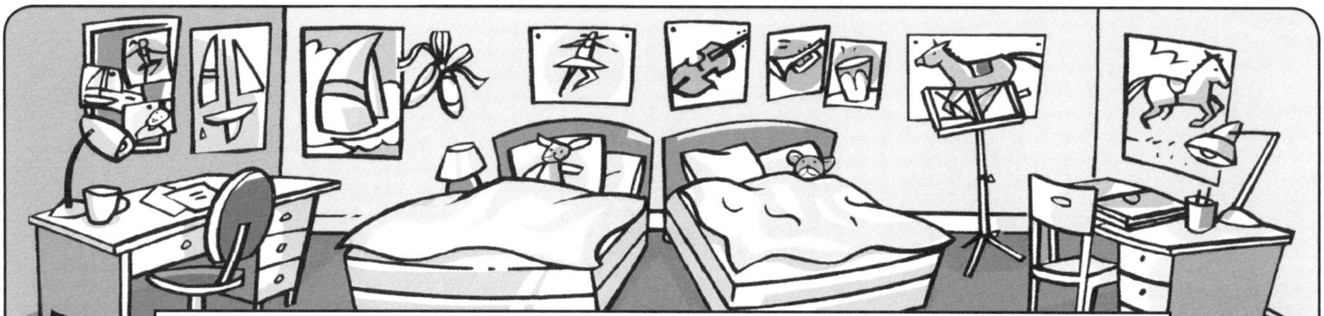

*Sophie et moi, **on ne s'entend pas. Elle ne s'intéresse pas** aux chevaux, et moi, je ne m'intéresse pas à la voile. **Elle ne s'intéresse pas** à la musique, et moi, **je ne m'intéresse pas** à la danse. C'est difficile, quand on partage une chambre!*

- With a negative reflexive verb, the negative phrase (for instance, *ne…pas*) goes around the group consisting of the reflexive pronoun and the verb:
  *On **ne** s'entend **pas**.* – We do**n't** get on.
  *Elle **ne** s'intéresse **pas** aux chevaux.* – She is**n't** interested in horses.
  *Je **ne** m'intéresse **pas** à la danse.* – I'm **not** interested in dance.
- The same happens with other negative phrases:
  *On **ne** s'entend **plus**.* – We do**n't** get on **any more**.

- Manon has got exams, and her lifestyle has changed.
  Rewrite each sentence in the negative, with the phrase provided.

1. *Manon s'amuse tout le week-end.* — *ne…pas*
   Exemple: Manon ne s'amuse pas tout le week-end.
2. *Manon se repose le dimanche.* — *ne…jamais*
3. *Elle se lève à 10 heures du matin.* — *ne…pas*
4. *Elle s'intéresse aux émissions de télé.* — *ne…plus*
5. *Elle se promène dans les magasins en ville.* — *ne…jamais*
6. *Manon dit: «Je me couche à 9 heures du soir.»* — *ne…pas*
7. *Manon et son frère se disputent.* — *ne…jamais*
8. *Manon dit: «Je m'entends bien avec ma meilleure amie.»* — *ne…pas*
9. *La sœur de Manon dit: «Tu te baignes à la plage.»* — *ne…jamais*
10. *Manon et ses amis se retrouvent au café.* — *ne…plus*
11. *La mère de Manon dit: «Tes amis et toi, vous vous voyez le soir.»* — *ne…pas*
12. *Manon dit: «Ma correspondante et moi, nous nous écrivons tous les jours.»* — *ne…plus*

Name:

Interrogative forms

- There are various ways of making a question from a statement.
  You can add *est-ce que ...?* at the start:
  Est-ce que *vous vendez des cannes à pêche?* – Do you sell fishing rods?
  You can leave the statement as it is, but raise your voice at the end:
  Vous vendez des cannes à pêche? – Do you sell fishing rods?
  You can swap the subject and the verb round (and add a hyphen between the two):
  Vendez-vous *des cannes à pêche?* – Do you sell fishing rods?
- Note that if the verb ends with a vowel, you add not just one hyphen, but *-t-*:
  A-t-il *des cannes à pêche?* – Has he got fishing rods?
  Y a-t-il *des cannes à pêche?* – Are there fishing rods?
- You can also use a question word such as *comment, quand, où, pourquoi, combien, combien de temps, à quelle heure, qui, qu'est-ce qui, qu'est-ce que.*

- A mother talks to her older children about a planned trip to the movies.
  On the back of this sheet, write three possible questions for each sentence.

1. *Vous allez au cinéma.*

Exemple Allez-vous au cinéma?

Exemple Vous allez au cinéma?

Exemple Est-ce que vous allez au cinéma?

2. *C'est un film de James Bond.*

3. *Il passe à l'Odéon.*

4. *Il est pour les moins de 18 ans.*

5. *Vous emmenez Mickaël.*

6. *Vous prenez la voiture.*

7. *Il y a de l'essence dans la voiture.*

8. *Vous rentrez avant minuit.*

Name:

Negative forms with interrogative forms

- A question can also be in the negative. If the question contains *est-ce que*, the negative words *ne...pas* go around the verb in the normal way:
  Pourquoi est-ce que tu ***ne*** *viens* ***pas****?* – Why don't you come in?
  Est-ce que l'eau ***n'****est* ***pas*** *assez chaude?* – Isn't the water warm enough?
- If the question contains a verb-pronoun inversion, i.e. if the verb (here, *est*) comes before the pronoun (here, *il*), *ne...pas* go around the group consisting of the verb and the pronoun:
  Pourquoi ***n'****est-il* ***pas*** *dans la valise?* – Why isn't it in the suitcase?

- Make these questions negative, then write the English equivalent.

1. *Pourquoi est-ce que tu appelles?* Exemple: Pourquoi est-ce que tu n'appelles pas?
   Exemple: Why don't you call?
2. *Pourquoi vient-il?* Exemple: Pourquoi ne vient-il pas?
   Exemple: Why isn't he coming?
3. *Qu'est-ce qu'elle mange?* ....
   ....
4. *Qu'est-ce qui coûte cher?* ....
   ....
5. *Qui est-ce qui part en vacances?* ....
   ....
6. *Est-ce que ce livre est trop dur?* ....
   ....
7. *Est-ce que vous prenez votre vélo?* ....
   ....
8. *Allez-vous au cinéma ce soir?* ....
   ....
9. *Qui a ses affaires de sport?* ....
   ....
10. *Pourquoi laissez-vous ce travail?* ....
    ....

Modes of address

- In French, young people use *tu* with their friends and family.
  *Maman, **tu as** de l'argent pour nous, **s'il te plaît**?* – Mum, **have you got** money for us, please?
  ***Tu aimes** les flippers, Fabien?* – **Do you like** pinball machines, Fabien?
- Young people use *vous* to adults they don't know so well, such as friends' parents or shop assistants.
  *Madame, est-ce que **vous avez** une serviette pour moi, **s'il vous plaît**?* – Mrs Dubois, **have you got** a towel for me, **please**?
- Adults use *tu* to young people treated as part of the family, but *vous* to strangers.
- *Vous* is also the plural form and is used by everyone to talk to more than one person.
  ***Vous rentrez** vers 6 heures, Théo et Fabien, c'est ça?* – **You're coming back** around 6pm, Théo and Fabien, is that right?

- Céline and her father are going shopping, taking Céline's friend, Audrey, with them.
  Fill in the blanks, using a *tu* or a *vous* form.

Papa: *On va dans quel magasin, Céline et Audrey? (aimer)* **1.** Exemple: Vous aimez *les Galeries Modernes?*

Céline et Audrey: *Oui, d'accord.*

Papa: *Céline, qu'est-ce que (acheter)* **2.** .... *aujourd'hui? Un pantalon?*

Céline: *Oui, et aussi des chaussures.*

Papa: *(vouloir)* **3.** .... *ce pantalon rose? Il est beau.*

Céline: *Papa, (ne pas comprendre)* **4.** .... *la mode. Il est horrible, ce pantalon!*

Qu'est-ce que (penser) **5.** .... *de ce pantalon, Audrey?*

Audrey: *Je suis d'accord avec* **6.** .... *, Céline. Rose, ce n'est pas très beau. Noir, c'est mieux.*

Céline: *Madame, vous avez ce pantalon en noir, s'il* **7.** .... *plaît?*

Shop assistant: *Oui, il existe en noir. (vouloir)* **8.** .... *l'essayer?*

Céline: *Oui, je veux bien. Et est-ce que (avoir)* **9.** .... *des chaussures?*

Shop assistant: *Pour les chaussures, (aller)* **10.** .... *là-bas.*

Papa: *Bien, les filles, je suis fatigué! On s'arrête au café. Qu'est-ce que (vouloir)* **11.** .... *boire?*

Céline: *Pour moi, un jus d'orange, s'il* **12.** .... *plaît, Papa.*

Papa: *Et toi, Audrey, qu'est-ce que (boire)* **13.** .... *?*

Audrey: *Une limonade, s'il* **14.** .... *plaît, monsieur.*

Name:

Impersonal verbs

- *Il faut* is a very useful set phrase meaning 'it is necessary to', 'you must', 'you have to', 'you need (to)'.
  It is invariable, which means it never changes.
  Il faut *huit œufs.* – **You need** eight eggs.
  Il faut *battre les œufs avec le sel.* – **You have to** whisk the eggs with the salt.

- Here is a list of problems. Find the best piece of advice at the bottom of the page, and write it out, using *il faut*.

1. *J'ai la grippe.* Exemple: Il faut prendre de l'aspirine.
2. *Ma voiture est en panne.* ....
3. *Le collège est vieux.* ....
4. *L'examen est difficile.* ....
5. *Je suis fatiguée.* ....
6. *Il y a des papiers dans les rues.* ....
7. *Les assiettes sont sales.* ....
8. *Mes cheveux sont trop longs.* ....
9. *C'est l'anniversaire de Lucas.* ....
10. *Il fait trop chaud.* ....
11. *J'ai faim.* ....
12. *Le frigo est vide.* ....

acheter un cadeau *aller chez le coiffeur* *faire la vaisselle*
faire les courses *installer des poubelles* *manger* *ouvrir la fenêtre* *prendre de l'aspirine*
repeindre les classes *se coucher tôt* *téléphoner au garage* *travailler dur*

Name:

Perfect tense with avoir 1

- To describe what happened in the past, you use the perfect tense. For most verbs, you use *avoir* + a form of the verb called the past participle. Here is the whole of the perfect tense for *manger* (to eat), a regular –*er* verb:
- To form the past participle, you add an ending to the stem of the verb.

j'ai mangé
tu as mangé
il/elle/on a mangé
nous avons mangé
vous avez mangé
ils/elles ont mangé

J'ai fini *le gâteau.* – **I finished** the cake.
Tu n'as pas attendu! – **You didn't wait**!
J'ai mangé *tous les biscuits aussi.* – **I ate** all the biscuits too

infinitive	stem	ending	past participle
regular –*er* verbs: *mang**er***	*mang-*	*-é*	*mangé*
regular –*ir* verbs: *fin**ir***	*fin-*	*-i*	*fini*
regular –*re* verbs: *attend**re***	*attend-*	*-u*	*attendu*

- Sarah tells the story of her grandmother's 80th birthday. Fill in the blanks with a verb in the perfect tense.

La semaine dernière, on (fêter) **1.** Exemple *a fêté* *les 80 ans de ma grand-mère. Mes parents (organiser)* **2.** .... *un anniversaire-surprise chez nous. D'abord, on (inviter)* **3.** .... *tous mes oncles, mes tantes et mes cousins. Ma mère (préparer)* **4.** .... *un bon repas et elle (finir)* **5.** .... *avec un gâteau délicieux. Moi, j' (choisir)* **6.** .... *le cadeau (un téléphone portable, parce qu'elle (perdre)* **7.** .... *son vieux téléphone), j' (décorer)* **8.** .... *la maison et j' (remplir)* **9.** .... *les vases de fleurs. Ensuite, cachés dans le séjour, on (attendre)* **10.** .... *À midi, ma grand-mère est entrée dans la maison: personne. Elle (regarder)* **11.** .... *dans le séjour – et mes cousins (commencer)* **12.** .... *à chanter 'Joyeux anniversaire'. Ma grand-mère (pleurer)* **13.** .... *un peu, et puis elle (répondre)* **14.** .... *: «Merci. Quelle bonne surprise!» Nous (parler)* **15.** .... *, nous (manger)* **16.** .... *et nous (passer)* **17.** .... *une très bonne journée ensemble.*

Name:

Perfect tense with avoir 2

- Some verbs have got an irregular past participle. You have to learn it by heart to be able to form the perfect tense.

*Mon père **a conduit** très vite.* – My father **drove** very fast.
*On **a dû** aller à l'hôpital.* – We **had to** go to hospital.

infinitive:	**perfect:**
avoir (to have)	*j'ai **eu***
boire (to drink)	*j'ai **bu***
conduire (to drive)	*j'ai **conduit***
courir (to run)	*j'ai **couru***
croire (to believe)	*j'ai **cru***
devoir (must, to have to)	*j'ai **dû***

- For each group of four sentences, choose the best verb and write it in the perfect tense in the blank.

A
1. *Coralie* ......**Exemple** a eu...... *une bonne note à son devoir.*
2. *Les garçons* .... *très vite pendant le marathon.*
3. *Kévin a perdu son téléphone portable. Il* .... *appeler d'une cabine.*
4. *Ils* .... *de l'eau minérale.*

avoir, boire, conduire, courir, devoir

B
1. *Le professeur* .... *mon excuse.*
2. *Tu* .... *un mail de Philippe?*
3. *J'* .... *une vraie moto hier.*
4. *Nous* .... *pour prendre le bus.*

avoir, boire, conduire, courir, croire

C
1. *Mes parents* .... *mon explication.*
2. *Tu* .... *mon frère à la gare?*
3. *Mon grand-père* .... *aller chez le docteur.*
4. *Vous* .... *du thé tous les jours?*

avoir, boire, conduire, croire, devoir

Name:

Perfect tense with avoir 3

- Some verbs have got an irregular past participle.
  You have to learn it by heart to be able to form the perfect tense.

  *Qu'est-ce que **vous avez fait** hier?* – What **did you do** yesterday?
  ***J'ai lu** des mails.* – **I read** e-mails.
  ***J'ai ouvert** des paquets.* – **I opened** parcels.

infinitive:	**perfect:**
dire (to say, to tell)	*j'ai* ***dit***
écrire (to write)	*j'ai* ***écrit***
être (to be)	*j'ai* ***été***
faire (to do, to make)	*j'ai* ***fait***
lire (to read)	*j'ai* ***lu***
mettre (to put)	*j'ai* ***mis***
ouvrir (to open)	*j'ai* ***ouvert***
pouvoir (can, to be able to)	*j'ai* ***pu***

- Renaud and the maths test.
  Put the words back in order, then translate the sentences into English.

1. *livres «Fermez de Michaud a maths» Monsieur dit vos*
   Exemple: Monsieur Michaud a dit «Fermez vos livres de maths». – Mr Michaud said, 'Close your maths books'.
2. *les Michaud questions écrit tableau Monsieur a au*
3. *questions tableau Les au élèves lu ont les*
4. *de genoux livre Renaud maths ses a sur mis le*
5. *le maths ouvert Renaud livre de a*
6. *réponse voir la Renaud a bonne pu*
7. *le ont devoir maths Les de élèves fait*
8. *avez les Michaud a réponses?» «Vous écrit Monsieur dit*
9. *le Renaud Monsieur devoir Michaud a de lu*
10. *fait Renaud?» le as Monsieur «Tu devoir seul, a Michaud écrit*
11. *j'ai «Non, le a livre» Renaud dit ouvert*
12. *a puni été Renaud*

Name:

Perfect tense with avoir 4

- Some verbs have got an irregular past participle. You have to learn it by heart to be able to form the perfect tense.

infinitive:	**perfect:**
prendre (to take)	*j'ai* ***pris***
recevoir (to receive, to get)	*j'ai* ***reçu***
rire (to laugh)	*j'ai* ***ri***
suivre (to follow)	*j'ai* ***suivi***
voir (to see)	*j'ai* ***vu***
vouloir (to want)	*j'ai* ***voulu***

Vous avez vu *les Zylbeks?* – **Did you see** the Zylbeks?
*Est-ce qu'****ils ont suivi*** *votre fusée?* – **Did they follow** your rocket?
Nous avons reçu *des cadeaux.* – **We got** some presents.

- In the perfect tense, *apprendre* (to learn) and *comprendre* (to understand) follow the same pattern as *prendre*.
Nous avons appris *beaucoup de choses.* – **We learnt** a lot.

- Youssef talks about his work experience in a zoo.
Fill in the blanks with a verb in the perfect tense.

- *Qu'est-ce que tu as fait pour ton stage en entreprise, Youssef?*
- *J'ai travaillé dans un zoo. Très intéressant! J' (apprendre)* **1.** Exemple ai appris *beaucoup de choses sur les animaux. J' (voir)* **2.** .... *des bébés hippopotames et des perroquets très rares. J' (vouloir)* **3.** .... *travailler avec les singes, parce qu'ils sont très intelligents. Les singes mangent des bananes, et d'autres fruits. Quand ils (voir)* **4.** .... *mon panier plein de bananes, ils m' (suivre)* **5.** .... *. J' (comprendre)* **6.** .... *: j'ai laissé mon panier par terre et un grand singe (prendre)* **7.** .... *les bananes. Après, j' (recevoir)* **8.** .... *une peau de banane sur la tête! Les singes (rire)* **9.** .... *enfin, je crois qu'ils (rire)* **10.** .... *. Moi aussi, j' (rire)* **11.** .... *. À la fin de mon stage, j' (recevoir)* **12.** .... *un certificat.*

Name:

Perfect tense with être

- To describe what happened in the past, you use the perfect tense. For most verbs, you use *avoir* + a form of the verb called the past participle. For some verbs, usually verbs of movement, you use *être*.
  ***Je suis allé** voir ce film.* – **I went** to see that film.
- With *être*, the past participle has to agree with the subject of the verb, i.e. the person or thing that does the action.

	masculine	feminine
singular	***Je suis allé** voir ce film.* – **I went** to see that film.	***Je suis allée** voir le dernier James Bond.* – **I went** to see the latest James Bond.
plural	***Nous sommes restés** jusqu'à la fin.* – **We stayed** till the end.	***Nous sommes entrées**.* – **We went in**.

- Here are the most common of those verbs. It is often helpful to think of MRS VANDERTRAMP – the name is made up of the first letters of the 14 verbs.

- Those ending in *–er* have a past participle in *–é*:

aller (to go)	*je suis all**é***
entrer (to go in)	*je suis entr**é***
rester (to stay)	*je suis rest**é***
monter (to go up)	*je suis mont**é***
arriver (to arrive)	*je suis arriv**é***
tomber (to fall)	*je suis tomb**é***
rentrer (to go back)	*je suis rentr**é***

- Other verbs have got different endings for their past participles:

partir (to leave)	*je suis part**i***
sortir (to go out)	*je suis sort**i***
descendre (to go down)	*je suis descend**u***
venir (to come)	*je suis ven**u***
revenir (to come back)	*je suis reven**u***
naître (to be born)	*je suis **né***
mourir (to die)	*il est **mort***

- Here is the full pattern:
  je suis allé(e)
  tu es allé(e)
  il est allé
  elle est allée
  nous sommes allé(e)s
  vous êtes allé(e)(s)
  ils sont allés
  elles sont allées

- With the polite *vous*, used to talk to one person you don't know well, there is no plural *s*:
  ***Vous êtes allé** au bureau des objets trouvés, monsieur?* – **Did you go** to the Lost Property Office, Sir?
  ***Vous êtes allée** au bureau des objets trouvés, madame?* – **Did you go** to the Lost Property Office, Madam?

- Pauline tells her teacher why she is late.
  Write the verb in the perfect tense in each blank. For each one, you have to decide:
  1. whether to use *être* or *avoir*; 2. if you use *être*, how to make the past participle agree.

\- *Pourquoi es-tu en retard, Pauline?*

\- *Ce matin, un oiseau (tomber)* **1.** Exemple est tombé *dans la cheminée de notre maison. J' (entendre)* **2.** Exemple ai entendu *un grand bruit, je (descendre)* **3.** .... *dans le séjour, j' (regarder)* **4.** .... *dans la cheminée et j' (voir)* **5.** .... *l'oiseau. Mes parents (appeler)* **6.** .... *les pompiers et moi, je (sortir)* **7.** .... *dans la rue. Très vite, les pompiers (arriver)* **8.** .... *. Ils (monter)* **9.** .... *sur le toit de la maison avec leur grande échelle. Ils (jeter)* **10.** .... *une petite échelle dans la cheminée et l'oiseau (sortir)* **11.** .... *L'oiseau (rester)* **12.** .... *immobile quelques minutes, mais il (ne pas mourir)* **13.** .... *Il (partir)* **14.** .... *et il (ne pas revenir)* **15.** .... *!*

Name:

Perfect tense of reflexive verbs

* *on a cambriolé* – there was a burglary at

- Reflexive verbs have two sets of personal pronouns.
  In the perfect tense, these verbs take *être* and the past participle agrees with the subject, i.e. the person or thing that does the action.
  Je me suis couchée *à 11 heures.* – **I went to bed** at 11pm.
  Nous nous sommes disputés. – **We argued**.
  Il s'est promené *en ville.* – **He went for a walk** in town.
- Here is the full pattern of *se coucher* (to go to bed):

je me suis couché(e)	*nous nous sommes couché(e)s*
tu t'es couché(e)	*vous vous êtes couché(e)(s)*
il s'est couché	*ils se sont couchés*
elle s'est couchée	*elles se sont couchées*

* *le traîneau* – sleigh

- Mathilde and her friend Jonathan have been on an unusual holiday to Lapland. Mathilde tells the story. The words are jumbled up. To find out what happened, put them in the right order.

1. *heures matin à suis me réveillée 5 du Je* — Exemple: Je me suis réveillée à 5 heures du matin.
2. *suis à 6 me heures Je levée* ....
3. *réveillé heures s' Jonathan à 6 est* ....
4. *est 7 Jonathan levé à heures s'* ....
5. *paresseux parce nous est Nous sommes qu'il disputés,* ....
6. *suis dans Je la lavée neige me* ....
7. *sommes en chien Nous traîneau* à nous promenés* ....
8. *baignés se l'eau dans chiens glacée Les sont* ....
9. *dans me un suis igloo Je reposée* ....
10. *amusés neige Nous dans sommes la nous* ....
11. *11 s'est heures Jonathan à couché* ....
12. *à suis me minuit Je couchée* ....

Name:

Imperfect tense of avoir and être

* With the <u>imperfect tense</u>, you can talk about the way things <u>used to be</u>, for instance in your childhood.
  *Quand **j'étais** petit, **nous n'avions pas** de maison.* – When **I was** small, **we didn't have** a house.
  ***Il n'y avait pas** d'électricité.* – **There was no** electricity. ***C'était** le luxe!* – **That was** luxury!

* *pauvres* – poor

* Here is the imperfect tense of *être* (to be) and *avoir* (to have).

*j'ét**ais***	*j'av**ais***
*tu ét**ais***	*tu av**ais***
*il/elle/on ét**ait***	*il/elle/on av**ait***
*nous ét**ions***	*nous av**ions***
*vous ét**iez***	*vous av**iez***
*ils/elles ét**aient***	*ils/elles av**aient***

* Note *c'était* – 'that was', 'it was'.
* Note *il y avait* – 'there was'.

---

* Grand-père talks about his childhood.
  For each blank, choose the correct imperfect form.

1. *Quand* Exemple j'étais *petit,* Exemple il y avait *un château ici.*
<u>il y avait</u> / <u>j'étais</u> / j'avais / nous avions

2. *Maintenant, c'est un supermarché. Avant,* .... *un cinéma.*
j'avais / c'était / il était

3. .... *huit dans la maison: ma grand-mère, mes parents, mes quatre frères et sœurs et moi.*
elle avait / ils étaient / nous étions

4. .... *des voitures dans les rues, mais pas beaucoup.*
nous avions / il y avait / il était

5. .... *de vrais étés, chauds et ensoleillés.*
on avait / ils étaient / nous étions

6. *Mes frères et sœurs et moi,* .... *tous un vélo.*
ils étaient / nous avions / j'avais

7. *Mes parents* .... *une vieille voiture, une Peugeot 301.*
il y avait / avaient / étaient

8. .... *scout et* .... *un uniforme.*
ils étaient / j'étais / c'était / j'avais

9. .... *de longues vacances en été, trois mois.*
nous étions / nous avions / il avait

10. *Ma grand-mère* .... *un petit chien noir, Médor.*
étaient / avions / avait

11. *Mon école* .... *petite, mais sympa.*
avait / était / avions

12. .... *heureux – pas riches, mais heureux.*
nous étions / il y avait / c'était

Name:

Imperfect tense of être and faire

- With the <u>imperfect tense</u>, you can talk about the way things <u>used to be</u>.
  Quand ***j'étais*** *jeune,* ***je faisais*** *du sport.* – When **I was** young, **I used to do** sport.
- Here is the imperfect tense of *être* (to be) and *faire* (to do, to make).

j'étais	*je faisais*
tu étais	*tu faisais*
il/elle/on était	*il/elle/on faisait*
nous étions	*nous faisions*
vous étiez	*vous faisiez*
ils/elles étaient	*ils/elles faisaient*

- Note *c'était* – 'that was', 'it was'.

- For each sentence, fill in the correct form of *faire* in the imperfect.

1. *Quand j'étais petite, je* ......Exemple *faisais*...... *du piano.*
faisais / fais/ faisions

2. *À 16 ans, ma fille* .... *les magasins tous les samedis.*
faisais / faisait / faites

3. *Quand nous étions à la campagne, nous* .... *beaucoup d'équitation.*
font / faisions / faisaient

4. *Vous* .... *du ski tous les week-ends en hiver?*
fait / faisais / faisiez

5. *Pour gagner de l'argent, je* .... *du babysitting.*
fais / faisais / font

6. *Qu'est-ce tu* .... *comme passe-temps, à 15 ans?*
faisons / faisait / faisais

7. *Mes enfants* .... *les courses, pour m'aider.*
faites / faisaient / font

8. *Si elle était malade, elle ne* .... *pas de sport.*
faisait / faire / faisiez

9. *Ils* .... *du tennis, mais seulement l'été.*
fais / faisons / faisaient

10. *Mon père* .... *du sport après le travail.*
faisait / font / faites

Name:

Imperfect tense of other verbs

* *un porte-plume et de l'encre* – pen-holder and ink

3

- With the <u>imperfect tense</u>, you can talk about the way things <u>used to be</u>, for instance in your childhood.
  On travaillait *dur, mais* ***on s'amusait*** *bien aussi.* – **We worked** hard, but **we had fun** too.
- With all verbs (except *être*), the imperfect is formed by removing the *-ons* from the *nous* form of the present tense and adding the imperfect endings. In these examples, the stem is underlined and the imperfect ending is in **bold:**
  *<u>travaill</u>ons – on <u>travaill</u>**ait*** (we worked)
  *<u>dur</u>ons – les vacances <u>dur</u>**aient*** (the holidays lasted)
  *<u>finiss</u>ons– l'école <u>finissons</u>**ait*** (school used to end)
  *<u>écriv</u>ons– on <u>ecri</u>**ait*** (we used to write)

- Write **P** for Past next to the sentences in the imperfect, and **N** for Now next to the sentences in the present.

1. *Les jeunes sortent souvent le samedi soir.* Exemple [N]
2. *Les cafés restaient ouverts tard.* Exemple [P]
3. *Les cinémas du centre-ville ferment.* [ ]
4. *En général, on choisissait un restaurant chinois.* [ ]
5. *On ne buvait pas d'alcool avant 21 ans.* [ ]
6. *Nous lisons des magazines de musique.* [ ]
7. *Vous organisez une fête tous les étés?* [ ]
8. *Le spectacle finissait à minuit.* [ ]
9. *Mes amis choisissent un plage sympa.* [ ]
10. *On prenait nos vélos pour aller en ville.* [ ]
11. *Ils venaient voir le cirque.* [ ]
12. *Elles vendent des glaces dans la rue.* [ ]
13. *L'été, on vivait dans le jardin.* [ ]
14. *Vous prenez l'avion ou le train?* [ ]

Name:

Contrasting tenses: perfect and imperfect

- With the imperfect tense, you can talk about the way things used to be. You can also use the imperfect to talk about an action that was going on in the past. In English, you might say 'I was –ing'. By contrast, you use the perfect tense for what happened while the other action was going on.
  Quand ***j'ai appris*** *la nouvelle,* ***je lisais*** *un livre.* – When **I learnt** the news, **I was reading** a book.
  Quand ***j'ai appris*** *la nouvelle,* ***je marchais*** *dans la rue.* – When **I learnt** the news, **I was walking** in the street.
  Je lisais *dans mon hamac quand une branche* ***est tombée*** *sur ma tête.* – **I was reading** in my hammock when a branch **fell** on my head.

- There are two verbs for each sentence, one in the imperfect and one in the perfect.
  Write each one in the correct gap.

1. Exemple Je marchais .... *sur la plage quand* Exemple j'ai vu .... *ma copine Audrey.*
   j'ai vu / je marchais
2. .... *une limonade quand* .... *le téléphone.*
   je buvais / j'ai entendu
3. *Mélanie* .... *une visite de Thomas pendant qu'elle* ....
   travaillait / a reçu
4. *Sophie* .... *pendant que mon père* .... *le dîner.*
   préparait / est arrivée
5. *Ma mère* .... *à l'aéroport; soudain, sa voiture* .... *en panne.*
   allait / est tombée
6. .... *des courses, mais* .... *ton porte-monnaie?*
   tu faisais / tu as perdu
7. *Le voleur* .... *pendant que la famille* ....
   dormait / est entré
8. *L'arbre* .... *pendant que la famille* .... *en vacances.*
   est tombé / était
9. *Elle* .... *parce qu'elle* ....
   avait faim / a mangé
10. *Vous* .... *parce que vous* .... ?
    étiez fatigués / êtes partis
11. *Elle* .... *dans la rivière quand elle* .... *un crocodile.*
    se baignait / a vu
12. *J'* .... *le piano quand* .... *six ans.*
    ai commencé / j'avais

Name:

Future tense with aller

- To talk about what is going to happen soon, or what you are planning to do soon, you use the immediate future. Just like in English, you use the correct part of the verb *aller* (to go) + infinitive (i.e. the dictionary form).
  Qu'est-ce que ***tu vas faire*** *ce week-end?* – What **are you going to do** this weekend?
  Je vais réparer *mon vélo.* – **I am going to repair** my bike. ***Nous allons faire*** *du ski.* – **We are going to go** skiing.
- With reflexive verbs, the reflexive pronoun comes between the correct part of the verb *aller* and the infinitive:
  Je vais me lever *à 8 heures.* – **I am going to get up** at 8 o'clock.
- To use or understand the immediate future, you need to know all forms of the verb *aller* in the present very well.

aller:

je vais	*nous allons*
tu vas	*vous allez*
il/elle/on va	*ils/elles vont*

- Write these sentences in the immediate future.

A

1. *nous – mettre des fleurs dans le jardin* — **Exemple** Nous allons mettre des fleurs dans le jardin.
2. *le professeur – lire les devoirs* ....
3. *mes parents – faire les magasins* ....
4. *vous – partir en vacances* ....
5. *tu – apprendre l'espagnol* ....
6. *elles – recevoir des cadeaux* ....
7. *je – prendre le train* ....
8. *le docteur – venir chez nous* ....

- Write these sentences in the immediate future. All the verbs are *–er* verbs, so the infinitive will be easy to find.

B

1. *Élodie commence le piano.* — **Exemple** Élodie va commencer le piano.
2. *Vous vous levez à 7 heures du matin?* ....
3. *Je mange une pizza.* ....
4. *Nous essayons le patinage sur glace.* ....
5. *Tu montes à la tour Eiffel?* ....
6. *Il aime ce chanteur.* ....
7. *Kévin et Alexandre jouent au tennis.* ....
8. *Ils se baignent avant le déjeuner.* ....

Name:

Future tense

- To talk about what will happen, or what you are planning to do in the distant future, you use the future tense.
  J'aurai *une grosse fusée et* ***j'irai*** *sur la Lune.* – **I will have** a big rocket and **I will go** to the Moon.
  Je pourrai *aller avec toi?* – **Will I be able** to go with you?
- Note that in English, after 'when', you use the present tense, but in French, after *quand*, you use the future tense:
  Quand je serai *grand,* ***j'aurai*** *une grosse fusée.* – **When I am** grown up, **I will have** a big rocket.
  Quand tu seras *grand, moi aussi,* ***je serai*** *grande.* – **When you are** grown up, **I will be** grown up too.
- The future tense of regular verbs is formed by adding the future tense endings, shown in **bold** below to the infinitive.
- Here is the future tense of *monter* and of some common irregular verbs.
  You might not have to use this tense, but it is useful to be able to recognise it.

monter (to go up):	***être*** (to be):	***avoir*** (to have)	***aller*** (to go)	***faire*** (to do, to make)
*je monter**ai***	*je ser**ai***	*j'aur**ai***	*j'ir**ai***	*je fer**ai***
*tu monter**as***	*tu ser**as***	*tu aur**as***	*tu ir**as***	*tu fer**as***
*il/elle/on monter**a***	*il/elle/on ser**a***	*il/elle/on aur**a***	*il/elle/on ir**a***	*il/elle/on fer**a***
*nous monter**ons***	*nous ser**ons***	*nous aur**ons***	*nous ir**ont***	*nous fer**ons***
*vous monter**ez***	*vous ser**ez***	*vous aur**ez***	*vous ir**ez***	*vous fer**ez***
*ils/elles monter**ont***	*ils/elles ser**ont***	*ils/elles aur**ont***	*ils/elles ir**ont***	*ils/elles fer**ont***

- Read Maxime's letter. Underline all the verbs in the future tense.

Exemple

Quand je serai grand, je serai astronaute. Quand j'étais petit, j'adorais les fusées. À la télé, je préférais regarder Thunderbirds. Pour devenir astronaute, il faut être bon en maths. Ce n'est pas un problème, parce que j'ai de bonnes notes. J'ai eu 20 à mon dernier devoir. D'abord, j'irai à l'université et j'étudierai la mécanique et l'aéronautique. Les études durent quatre ans. Ensuite, j'entrerai dans l'armée de l'air. Mon père et ma mère sont déjà dans l'armée, alors je connais bien ce métier. On me donnera un bel uniforme, et mes parents seront contents! Je pense que je ferai beaucoup de sport, et de l'entraînement tous les jours. La natation, le cyclisme et le jogging sont tous des sports utiles. Je me préparerai très bien. Quand on me choisira pour une mission, j'espère aller sur la Lune, et peut-être sur Mars.

Name:

Conditional tense

- The conditional tense is formed by adding the conditional endings, shown in **bold** on the right, in place of the future endings. *Je voudrais* and *j'aimerais* are conditional forms of *vouloir* (to want) and *aimer* (to like, to love) meaning 'I would like', 'I'd like'. Here are the other persons in the pattern:

*je voudr**ais***	*j'aimer**ais***
*tu voudr**ais***	*tu aimer**ais***
*il/elle/on voudr**ait***	*il/elle/on aimer**ait***
*nous voudr**ions***	*nous aimer**ions***
*vous voudr**iez***	*vous aimer**iez***
*ils/elles voudr**aient***	*ils/elles aimer**aient***

*Pierre **voudrait** une PlayStation.* – Pierre **would like** a PlayStation.
*Marine **aimerait** avoir une poupée qui parle.* – Marine **would like** to have a speaking doll.
*Mickaël et Antoine **voudraient** une boîte de Lego.* – Mickaël and Antoine **would like** a box of Lego.
*Amandine et Laetitia **aimeraient** aller à Disneyland.* – Amandine and Laetitia **would like** to go to Disneyland.
***Je voudrais** un ordinateur pour mon travail.* – **I would like** a computer for my work.

- Translate the English sentences by completing the French ones. You can use either *aimer* or *vouloir*.

1. She would like to listen to this CD. **Exemple** Elle voudrait/aimerait .... *écouter ce disque.*
2. My parents would like a smaller house. .... *une maison plus petite.*
3. I would like to visit Paris. .... *visiter Paris.*
4. Nicolas would like a mountain bike. .... *un VTT.*
5. We would like to go out on Saturday night. .... *sortir samedi soir.*
6. Would you like to come with me? *Est-ce que* .... *venir avec moi?*
7. We would like to know the end of the story. .... *connaître la fin de l'histoire.*
8. They would like to go away on holiday. .... *partir en vacances.*
9. Clara would like to be a doctor. .... *être médecin.*
10. Would you like to become a millionaire? .... *devenir millionnaire?*
11. They would like a new car. .... *une voiture neuve.*
12. He would like sugar in his coffee. .... *du sucre dans son café.*

Name:

Pluperfect tense

* *la retenue* – detention

- You use a verb in the <u>pluperfect tense</u> to talk about a past action which is further back in time than another past action.
- In this example, 'not doing homework' happened before 'staying in detention' – which is in the imperfect:
  *Quand **nous n'avions pas fait** nos devoirs, nous restions en retenue.* – When **we hadn't done** our homework, we used to stay in detention.
- In this example, 'having a detention' happened before 'not telling' – which is in the perfect tense:
  *Tu ne m'as pas dit que **tu avais eu** une retenue!* – You didn't tell me that **you'd had** a detention!
- The pluperfect is formed like the perfect, but *avoir* (or *être*) are in the imperfect instead of the present.
  This is similar to English.

perfect:	*J'ai fait mes devoirs.* – I have done my homework.
	Je suis parti en vacances. – I went on holiday.
pluperfect:	*J'avais fait mes devoirs.* – I had done my homework.
	J'étais parti en vacances. – I had gone on holiday.

- In each sentence, underline the verb in the pluperfect.

Exemple
1. *Je pensais que <u>tu avais compris</u>.*
2. *Elle avait marché longtemps et elle était fatiguée.*
3. *J'ai écouté le disque que tu m'avais recommandé.*
4. *Ils avaient étudié le chinois avant de partir en Chine.*
5. *Thomas a pleuré parce qu'il avait cassé sa petite voiture.*
6. *Romain avait réussi à son examen, alors il a reçu un cadeau.*
7. *J'avais travaillé dur et je voulais partir en vacances.*
8. *Anaïs m'avait donné son numéro, mais je l'ai perdu.*
9. *Vous avez lu le livre que je vous avais donné?*
10. *Ils avaient perdu leur chemin, alors ils sont entrés dans le café.*
11. *Sophie a dit qu'elle avait gagné à la Loterie.*
12. *Elles ont regardé le film qui avait eu un Oscar.*

Name:

Imperative 1

- A verb in the imperative is used to give an order. The singular form is used to talk to one person (to a young person or someone familiar), the plural to several people, or to one unfamiliar adult. The plural is always the same as the *vous* form of the present tense. The singular is often the same as the *tu* form of the present tense, but with *–er* verbs and *aller*, the final *–s* is dropped. Here are imperative forms of *écouter* (to listen) and *venir* (to come).
  Écoute! – **Listen!** (singular)
  Venez! – **Come!** (plural)
- Note what happens to reflexive verbs such as *se dépêcher* (to hurry up) or *s'asseoir* (to sit down):
  Dépêche-toi! – **Hurry up!** (singular)
  Asseyez-vous! – **Sit down!** (plural)

	regular *–er* **verbs:** ***écouter*** (to listen)	**regular** *–ir* **verbs:** ***choisir*** (to choose)	**regular** *–re* **verbs:** ***répondre*** (to answer)	**reflexive verbs:** ***se lever*** (to get up)	**irregular verb:** ***aller*** (to go)	**irregular verb:** ***faire*** (to do, to make)	**irregular verb:** ***mettre*** (to put)
singular **plural**	*Écoute!* *Écoutez!*	*Choisis!* *Choisissez!*	*Réponds!* *Répondez!*	*Lève-toi!* *Levez-vous!*	*Va!* *Allez!*	*Fais!* *Faites!*	*Mets!* *Mettez!*

- Put each sentence into the imperative.

1. *Benjamin doit choisir un pantalon.* **Exemple** Choisis un pantalon! ....
2. *Aurélie doit finir le devoir de maths.* ....
3. *Monsieur et Madame Fourcade doivent monter dans le taxi.* ....
4. *Le docteur dit à Monsieur Joliot de s'asseoir.* ....
5. *Émilie doit se laver.* ....
6. *Le chien Pivert doit manger sa viande.* ....
7. *Alexandre doit attendre le bus.* ....
8. *Mathieu doit répondre au professeur.* ....
9. *Les enfants doivent se coucher.* ....
10. *Sa mère dit à David de mettre les assiettes sur la table.* ....
11. *Son père dit à Céline de faire son lit.* ....
12. *Coralie et Simon doivent se baigner dans la piscine.* ....

Name:

Imperative 2

- A verb in the imperative is used to give an order. In the negative, *ne ... pas* go either side of the verb:
  ***Ne pleure pas**, Céline.* – **Don't cry**, Céline.
- Note the word order with a reflexive verb, here *s'asseoir*, 'to sit down', and *se disputer*, 'to argue'.
  ***Asseyez-vous**.* – **Sit down**.
  ***Ne vous disputez pas**, les enfants.* – **Don't argue**, children.
- Direct object pronouns and indirect object pronouns are attached to the imperative with a hyphen. The indirect pronoun for 'to me' takes the form *moi* (called the emphatic form).
  ***Donne-le** à Popi.* – **Give it** to Popi. (direct object pronoun)
  ***Donne-moi** le gâteau!* – Give me the cake! (= 'Give the cake to me': indirect object pronoun)
  ***Donne-le-moi**!* – **Give it to me**! (direct and indirect object pronouns)
- *Lui* is the indirect object pronoun for 'to him' or 'to her'. *Leur* stands for 'to them'.
  ***Ne lui donne pas**, Maman.* – **Don't give (it) to her**, Mum.
  ***Ne leur donne pas** ce gâteau, Brigitte.* – **Don't give them** that cake, Brigitte.

- For each sentence, choose which of the two options is the most appropriate.

1. *Les enfants ne doivent pas prendre l'ascenseur.*	*Ne prends pas l'ascenseur! / Ne prenez pas l'ascenseur!* Exemple
2. *Jérémy demande l'explication du problème.*	*Explique-moi le problème! / Explique-leur le problème!*
3. *La plage est dangereuse le soir.*	*Ne vous promenez pas sur la plage! / Ne leur promenez pas sur la plage!*
4. *Les élèves doivent répondre au professeur.*	*Répondez-la! / Répondez-lui!*
5. *Julie veut prendre le livre de Maxime.*	*Ne prends le pas! / Ne le prends pas!*
6. *Maman n'aime pas les roses.*	*Ne lui achète pas de roses! / N'achète-lui pas de roses!*
7. *Papa ne veut pas de cravate.*	*Ne le donne pas de cravate! / Ne lui donne pas de cravate!*
8. *Nicolas doit vite téléphoner à Audrey.*	*Téléphone-la vite! / Téléphone-lui vite!*
9. *Anaïs demande un CD à son grand-père.*	*Achète-moi ce CD, s'il te plaît! / Achète-me ce CD, s'il te plaît!*
10. *La rivière est sale.*	*Ne te baigne pas dans la rivière! / Ne baigne te pas dans la rivière!*
11. *On ne doit pas parler aux élèves pendant l'examen.*	*Ne les parlez pas! / Ne leur parlez pas!*
12. *Clément te demande son ballon.*	*Donne-le-moi! / Donne-te-moi!*

Passive voice

- Just like in English, you use a verb in the passive voice to say that something (or somebody) is having something done to them.
  Les insectes ***mangent*** *le suc des fleurs.* – Insects eat the juice of flowers. (active voice)
  Les insectes ***sont mangés*** *par les oiseaux.* – Insects are eaten by birds. (passive voice)
- Remember that the past participle agrees with the subject, just like an adjective.
  L'*oiseau est* ***mangé***. – The bird is eaten.
  Les *oiseaux sont* ***mangés***. – The birds are eaten.

- The words in the French sentences are jumbled up. Put them in the right order.

1. *pour payé euros voiture Je laver dix la suis* — **Exemple** Je suis payé dix euros pour laver la voiture.
2. *faits, vous sortir Si pouvez vos sont devoirs* ....
3. *cherche maintenant des je robe est chaussures La achetée;* ....
4. *qu'est-ce est faire? Si qu'on va la perdue, clef* ....
5. *sont général, préparés à les la En repas cuisine* ....
6. *repeinte cantine jaune La est en* ....
7. *tu par es film? choqué Est-ce que ce* ....
8. *l'école les finis, peut travaux ouvrir Si sont* ....
9. *par mangés les pandas Les sont bambous* ....
10. *surtout est Le visité l'été château* ....
11. *sont polluées l'usine Les par rivières* ....
12. *distribuées 10 Les le à lettres sont matin heures* ....

Name:

Present participle

La voiture **étant** très ancienne, elle est tombée en panne.

- The present participle is the form of a verb which ends in *–ant*. It is invariable: it never changes. It isn't often used in spoken language, but it is useful to be able to recognise it in written texts.
  *La voiture **étant** très ancienne, elle est tombée en panne.* – The car **being** very old, it broke down. / As the car was very old, it broke down.
- Most present participles are formed by adding *–ant* to the stem of the *nous* form of the present tense (the stem is in **bold** in the example below):
  aimer (to like, to love) – *nous **aim**ons* – *aimant*
- The three most important exceptions are:
  être (to be) – *étant*
  avoir (to have) – *ayant*
  savoir (to know) – *sachant*

- For each sentence, choose the present participle which makes most sense.

Exemple

1.	...Étant... *malade, elle est restée chez elle.*	*connaissant / ayant / étant*
2.	*Les nageurs* .... *un bracelet jaune doivent sortir de la piscine.*	*sachant / ayant / dormant*
3.	*Ne* .... *pas où est la gare, ils prennent un taxi.*	*sachant / voulant / pensant*
4.	.... *bien la ville, elle travaille comme guide pour touristes.*	*dormant / connaissant / voulant*
5.	*La bibliothèque* .... *fermée, il doit garder ses livres.*	*dormant / étant / sachant*
6.	.... *dans son hamac, il n'entend pas les enfants.*	*habitant / voyant / dormant*
7.	*Érika,* .... *sur la côte d'Azur, est habituée au soleil.*	*habitant / sachant / voulant*
8.	*Amandine,* .... *que son amie vient, fait un gros gâteau.*	*étant / ayant / pensant*
9.	.... *l'accident, l'homme a appelé la police.*	*voulant / étant / voyant*
10.	.... *acheter du lait, Vincent est entré dans le magasin.*	*dormant / voulant / habitant*

Name:

Expressions with avoir

- The verb *avoir* is used in many common set phrases.

avoir l'air (de) – to look (like)
avoir (15) ans – to be (15) years old
avoir besoin – to need
avoir de la chance – to be lucky
avoir chaud – to feel hot
avoir cours – to have a class
avoir envie de – to feel like/want
avoir faim – to be hungry
avoir froid – to be cold
avoir mal (à la tête) – to have a (head)ache
avoir peur – to be afraid
avoir raison – to be right
avoir soif – to be thirsty
avoir tort – to be wrong

***Tu as l'air** content.* – **You look** pleased.
***Je n'ai pas envie d'**aller au stade.* – **I don't feel like** going to the sports ground.
*Le prof **n'a pas l'air d'**être malade.* – The teacher **doesn't look as if** he was ill.

- Here is the present tense of the verb *avoir*:

j'ai
tu as
il/elle/on a
nous avons
vous avez
ils/elles ont

- Read Guillaume's story.
Fill in each blank with the correct form of an *avoir* phrase.

*J'***1.** Exemple ai *18* Exemple ans *, et j'***2.** .... *de partir en Afrique. Pourquoi?*

Parce qu'en Afrique, les gens sont pauvres et **3.** .... *d'aide. Ici en Europe, nous* **4.** ....

*Nous avons assez à manger et nous n'***5.** .... *pas* .... *. Nous avons de l'eau propre et*

*nous n'***6.** .... *pas* .... *. Le climat est tempéré et nous n'***7.** .... *pas*

souvent .... *. Par contre, en Afrique, il n'y a pas assez à manger et des millions de personnes*

8. .... *. Quand elles* **9.** .... *, elles boivent de l'eau sale. À cause de l'eau sale, elles*

10. .... *au ventre et elles tombent malades. En plus, ces personnes* **11.** .... *,*

parce qu'il y a souvent la guerre. Mes parents me disent «Tu **12.** .... *, Guillaume. Va d'abord à l'université.*

Ensuite, tu peux partir en Afrique.» C'est vrai, ça **13.** .... *dangereux. Mais je n'***14.** ....

pas .... *. Je pense que j'***15.** .... *de partir maintenant. Je peux toujours aller*

à l'université plus tard.

Name:

Expressions with faire

- The verb *faire* is used in many common set phrases:

Daily tasks
faire du babysitting – to do babysitting
faire les courses – to do the shopping
faire la cuisine – to do the cooking
faire les devoirs – to do homework
faire les magasins – to go around the shops
faire le ménage – to clean (around the house)
faire la queue – to queue up
faire la vaisselle – to wash up

Pastimes
faire du sport – to do sport
faire de la musique – to do music
faire du cricket – to play cricket
faire de la flûte – to play the flute
faire du judo – to do judo
faire du ski – to go skiing
faire du camping – to go camping

- *Il fait* is used as a set phrase to talk about the weather:

il fait mauvais – the weather's bad
il fait beau – the weather's fine
il fait froid – it is cold
il fait chaud – it is hot
il fait du soleil – it is sunny
il fait du vent – it is windy

- Here are all the forms of the verb *faire* in the present tense:

je fais	*nous faisons*
tu fais	*vous faites*
il/elle/on fait	*ils/elles font*

* *le cerf-volant* – kite

3

- This is what some people do, according to the weather. Fill in the blanks.

1. *Quand il* ..Exemple.. fait beau.., *Clémence* ..Exemple.. fait du sport.. . — *faire du sport / faire beau*
2. *Quand il* ...., *ma grand-mère* .... — *faire chaud / faire de la natation*
3. *Quand il* ...., *Anthony* .... — *faire de la flûte / faire mauvais*
4. *Quand il* ...., *nous* .... — *faire du soleil / faire de la l'athlétisme*
5. *Quand il* ...., *vous* .... ? — *faire du vent / faire du deltaplane*
6. *Quand il* ...., *mes amies* .... — *faire les magasins / faire froid*
7. *Quand il* ...., *tu* .... ? — *faire du cricket / faire chaud*
8. *Quand il* ...., *Jonathan* .... — *faire du soleil / faire du bateau*
9. *Quand il* ...., *je* .... — *faire du camping / faire beau*
10. *Quand il* ...., *Mathilde* .... — *faire du piano / faire mauvais*
11. *Quand il* ...., *Léo et* .... — *faire froid / faire du ski*
12. *Quand il* ...., *nous* .... — *faire du vent / faire du cerf-volant**

Name:

à and de + definite article

- *Jouer à* is used to talk about a sport. With a masculine noun like *le rugby*, you use *jouer au*. With a plural word (*les*), you use *jouer aux*.
  Florian ***joue au*** *rugby.* – Florian **plays** rugby.
- *Jouer de* is used to talk about a musical instrument. With a masculine noun like *le piano*, you use *jouer du* and with a feminine noun like *la guitare*, you use *jouer de la*.
  Il préfère ***jouer du*** *piano.* – He prefers **playing the** piano.
  Il aime ***jouer de la*** *guitare.* – He likes **playing the** guitar.
- Remember the present tense of regular *–er* verbs:

je joue	*nous jouons*
tu joues	*vous jouez*
il/elle/on joue	*ils/elles jouent*

le basket
la batterie
le cricket
les échecs
la flûte
le foot
le golf
la guitare
le hockey
le piano
le ping-pong
le rugby
le synthé
le tennis

- The manager of a leisure centre talks about the range of activities available. Fill in the blanks.

Au centre de vacances Forme et Loisirs, il y a beaucoup de choses à faire. On peut faire des sports d'équipe, et

Exemple
1. ....jouer au.... *foot. On peut aussi* **2.** .... *rugby. Nous avons une grande salle omnisports. Quand il pleut, les jeunes* **3.** .... *hockey, ou ils* **4.** .... *basket. Il n'y a pas seulement les sports d'équipe. Beaucoup de jeunes* **5.** .... *tennis, et certains* **6.** .... *ping-pong. Mais on peut aussi faire d'autres activités. Il y a des cours pour les jeunes qui veulent* **7.** .... *batterie. Il y a des jeunes qui* **8.** .... *piano, et d'autres qui* **9.** .... *guitare. Il y a même un petit groupe qui* **10.** .... *flûte, et qui veut apprendre à* **11.** .... *synthé. Certains* **12.** .... *échecs. Est-ce qu'il y a des choses qui ne sont pas possibles? Eh bien, personne ne* **13.** .... *golf, mais cette année, un groupe de visiteurs anglais* **14.** .... *cricket.*

Name:

à + town and en/au + country

- When talking about places you go to, you use the prepositions *à* with names of towns (*Venise, Paris*), *en* with feminine countries (*la Turquie, la France, l'Angleterre*), *au* with masculine countries (*le Zimbabwe*) and *aux* with plural countries (*les Etats-Unis).*
  *Je vais **en Turquie**, puis **à Venise**, puis **au Zimbabwe**.* – I'm going **to Turkey**, then **to Venice**, then **to Zimbabwe**.
- You use the same prepositions to say that you live or stay in those places.
  *J'habite **en Turquie**.* – I live **in Turkey**.
  *J'habite **à Venise**.* - I live **in Venice**.
  *J'habite **au Zimbabwe**.* - I live **in Zimbabwe**.
- In front of words like *ville* (town) or *pays* (country), you always use *dans* (to, in).
  *Je vais **dans** une grande ville.* – I'm going **to** a large town.
  *J'habite **dans** un petit pays.* – I live **in** a small country.

l'Amérique ***f***
la Belgique
le Canada
le Luxembourg

- Read this letter from Thomas, a French Canadian boy.
  Fill in the gaps with the correct preposition.

Nous habitons **1.** ......Exemple: au...... *Canada, plus précisément* **2.** .... *Québec,* **3.** ....

une petite ville, Saint-Philémon. **4.** .... *Saint-Philémon, il n'y a pas grand-chose à faire en été.*

Mais en hiver, les touristes viennent **5.** .... *Saint-Philémon pour faire du ski. Nous parlons français, alors*

nous aimons aller **6.** .... *France. Nous allons souvent* **7.** .... *Paris.* **8.** ....

une grande ville comme Paris, il y a beaucoup de choses à faire. Nous allons aussi **9.** .... *Belgique, par*

exemple **10.** .... *Bruxelles, et même* **11.** .... *Luxembourg, un très petit pays.*

Nous connaissons Londres, car ma grand-mère habite **12.** .... *Angleterre. Mais l'Europe, c'est loin,*

alors nous allons souvent **13.** .... *États-Unis. J'ai des cousins* **14.** .... *New York.*

Quelquefois, je vais **15.** .... *Seattle pour voir ma tante. Nous allons régulièrement* **16.** ....

Montréal. **17.** .... *Amérique aussi, il y a des villes intéressantes!*

Name:

Prepositions 1

- You use these prepositions and adverbs to talk about where something is.

Prepositions:	**Adverbs:**
dans – in	*dedans* – inside
derrière – behind	*dehors* – outside
devant – in front of	
entre – between	
sous – under	
sur – on	*Le jardin est* ***dans*** *la maison.* – The garden is **in** the house.
vers – towards	*Les chambres et la cuisine sont* ***dehors***. – The bedrooms and the kitchen are **outside**.

- The estate agent carries on showing his client round the property. Fill in the gaps with a preposition or an adverb from the list.

1. *La machine à laver est* Exemple dans .... *la salle de bains.*
2. .... *l'escalier, voici un placard pour les chaussures.*
3. *Les toilettes sont* .... *la salle de bains et la chambre.*
4. *Le téléphone est* .... *cette petite table.*
5. *Il fait toujours chaud* .... *la véranda.*
6. .... *la maison, il y a un petit jardin.*
7. .... *, il y a une balançoire et un toboggan.*
8. *On ne voit pas la piscine de la rue: elle est* .... *les arbres.*
9. *Voici la piscine. Attention: il n'y a pas d'eau* ....
10. *Les magasins? Allez* .... *la plage, et les magasins sont à gauche.*
11. .... *, il y a un barbecue.*
12. *Il existe une petite cave* .... *la maison.*

Name:

Prepositions 2

- Prepositions ending in *de* or *à* may need to adjust to the noun that follows:
  Allez ***jusqu'au*** *supermarché.* – Go **as far as the** supermarket. (*le supermarché*)
  La fontaine est ***au milieu de la*** *place.* – The fountain is **in the middle of the** square. (*la place*)
  en face du *supermarché* – **opposite the** supermarket (*le supermarché*)
  à côté de l'*office de tourisme* – **near the** tourist office (*l'office de tourisme*)

à côté de – next to
au bord de – by the side of
au bout de – at the end of
au fond de – at the bottom of
au milieu de – in the middle of
autour de – around
en bas de – in the lower part of
en haut de – at the top of
en face de – opposite
de l'autre côté de – on the other side of
loin de – far from
près de – near
jusqu'à – as far as

- A tourist brochure describes attractions around the town of Saint-Médard.
  For each sentence, choose the best preposition from the list.

A **1.** *Il y a un lac* ....Exemple près de.......... *Saint-Médard.*
2. *On peut pique-niquer* .... *lac.*
3. *Si on loue un bateau, on peut visiter l'île* .... *lac.*
4. *On peut se promener* .... *île.*
5. .... *lac, on peut voir des poissons.*

B **1.** .... *lac, il y a un café.*
2. .... *café, il y a une route.*
3. .... *route, il y a une tour ancienne.*
4. *C'est intéressant d'aller* .... *tour.*

C **1.** *La tour n'est pas* .... *lac: 500 mètres.*
2. .... *tour, il y a un drapeau.*
3. .... *tour, il y a une porte.*
4. .... *tour, on voit de grands arbres.*

A
au bord de
au fond de
au milieu de
autour de
en haut de
~~*près de*~~

B
à côté de
au bout de
au fond de
en face de
jusqu'à

C
de l'autre côté de
en bas de
en haut de
jusqu'à
loin de

Name:

Means of transport

- All means of transport can take the preposition *en*, except *à pied*, 'on foot', 'walking'.
  ***À pied**, c'est plus rapide qu'**en voiture**!* – **Walking** is faster than **driving**!

en train – by train
en car – by coach
en bus – by bus
en bateau – by boat
en moto – by motorbike

on y va en voiture – we're driving there
on y va en avion – we're flying there
on y va en vélo – we're cycling there
on y va à pied – we're walking there

- For each situation, choose the most appropriate means of transport.

A
1. *Paris-Londres, pour le travail* — J'y vais ......(Exemple) en train...... .
2. *Calais-Douvres* — J'y vais ....
3. *Paris-Bordeaux, seul* — J'y vais ....

A: *bateau, moto, ~~train~~, vélo*

B
1. *Paris-Bordeaux, avec ma famille* — J'y vais ....
2. *la plage, à un kilomètre* — J'y vais ....
3. *Paris-New York, pour le travail* — J'y vais ....

B: *avion, bus, pied, voiture*

C
1. *Paris-Londres, pour un voyage de classe* — J'y vais ....
2. *le collège, à dix kilomètres* — J'y vais ....
3. *les magasins, à deux kilomètres* — J'y vais ....

C: *avion, bus, car, vélo*

D
1. *Londres-Washington* — J'y vais ....
2. *la piscine, à un kilomètre* — J'y vais ....
3. *le grand magasin, avec ma sœur et ma mère* — J'y vais ....

D: *bus, train, vélo, avion*

Name:

Prepositions 3

- Here are some useful prepositions:

avant – before
après – after
chez – at (someone's) house
contre – against
par – by
pour – for
sans – without
sauf – except

Je mange tout, ***sauf*** *le poulet, les frites, la salade et les pommes.* – I eat everything, **except** chicken, chips, salad and apples.

- In these statements about Quentin's school life, the preposition is missing. Fill in the gaps with one of the prepositions listed above.

1. *Je rentre à la maison* Exemple ......après...... *les cours.*
2. *Je travaille dur* .... *les examens.*
3. *J'aime toutes les matières,* .... *la géographie.*
4. *On ne peut pas trouver de travail* .... *diplôme.*
5. *Pour les maths, je suis aidé* .... *ma grande sœur.*
6. *Quelquefois, je vais* .... *mon copain Mathieu pour faire mes devoirs.*
7. *Mon ordinateur est en panne; c'est difficile de travailler* .... *ordinateur.*
8. *Le week-end, je vais* .... *mon père.*
9. *Je suis* .... *l'uniforme scolaire – c'est pénible.*
10. .... *les sportifs, il y a un stade, au collège.*
11. .... *les examens, on va visiter une villa romaine.*
12. *La visite est organisée* .... *le prof d'histoire.*

Name:

Adjectives + de or à

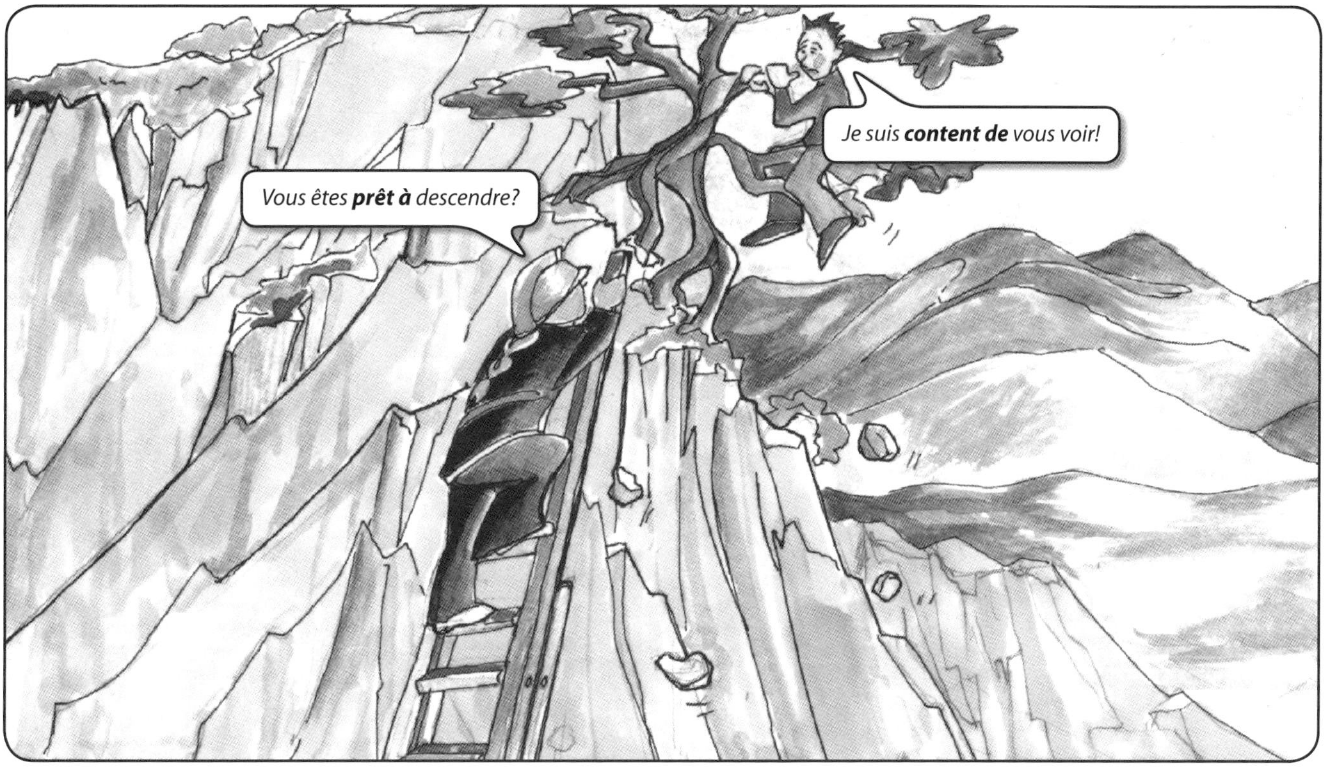

- Many adjectives can be followed by *de* + verb in the infinitive (the dictionary form of the verb).
  *Je suis **content de** vous voir!* – I am **pleased to** see you!
- A few adjectives can be followed by *à* + verb in the infinitive.
  *Vous êtes **prêt à** descendre?* – Are you **ready to** come down?
  Here are the most common ones:
  prêt(e) à – ready to
  le dernier/la dernière à – the last to
  le premier/la première à – the first to
  le seul/la seule à – the only one to

- Anaïs talks about her friend Adèle and her motorbike.
  Fill the gaps with an adjective from the list below, adding *de* (*d'*) or *à* as appropriate.

Ma copine Adèle est **1.** Exemple la seule à *avoir une moto. Moi, je suis toujours* **2.** .... *monter sur sa moto. Pour nous, il est* **3.** .... *aller au cinéma. L'été, il est* **4.** .... *aller à la plage. Nous habitons dans un petit village; sans la moto d'Adèle, il est* **5.** .... *sortir le soir. Adèle est sympa – elle est toujours* **6.** .... *emmener un copain ou une copine. Elle est* **7.** .... *téléphoner aux copains, le samedi. Mais il faut faire attention, bien sûr. Il est* **8.** .... *conduire une moto quand on est fatigué. Il est* **9.** .... *être prudent sur la route. En plus, Adèle est souvent* **10.** .... *arriver en classe, parce que la moto tombe souvent en panne. Moi aussi, j'aimerais avoir une moto. Je suis* **11.** .... *travailler cet été pour gagner de l'argent. Il y a beaucoup de tourisme l'ete, alors c'est* **12.** .... *trouver du travail.*

contente dangereux la dernière facile
important impossible possible la première prête la seule

Name:

Verbs taking à or de + infinitive

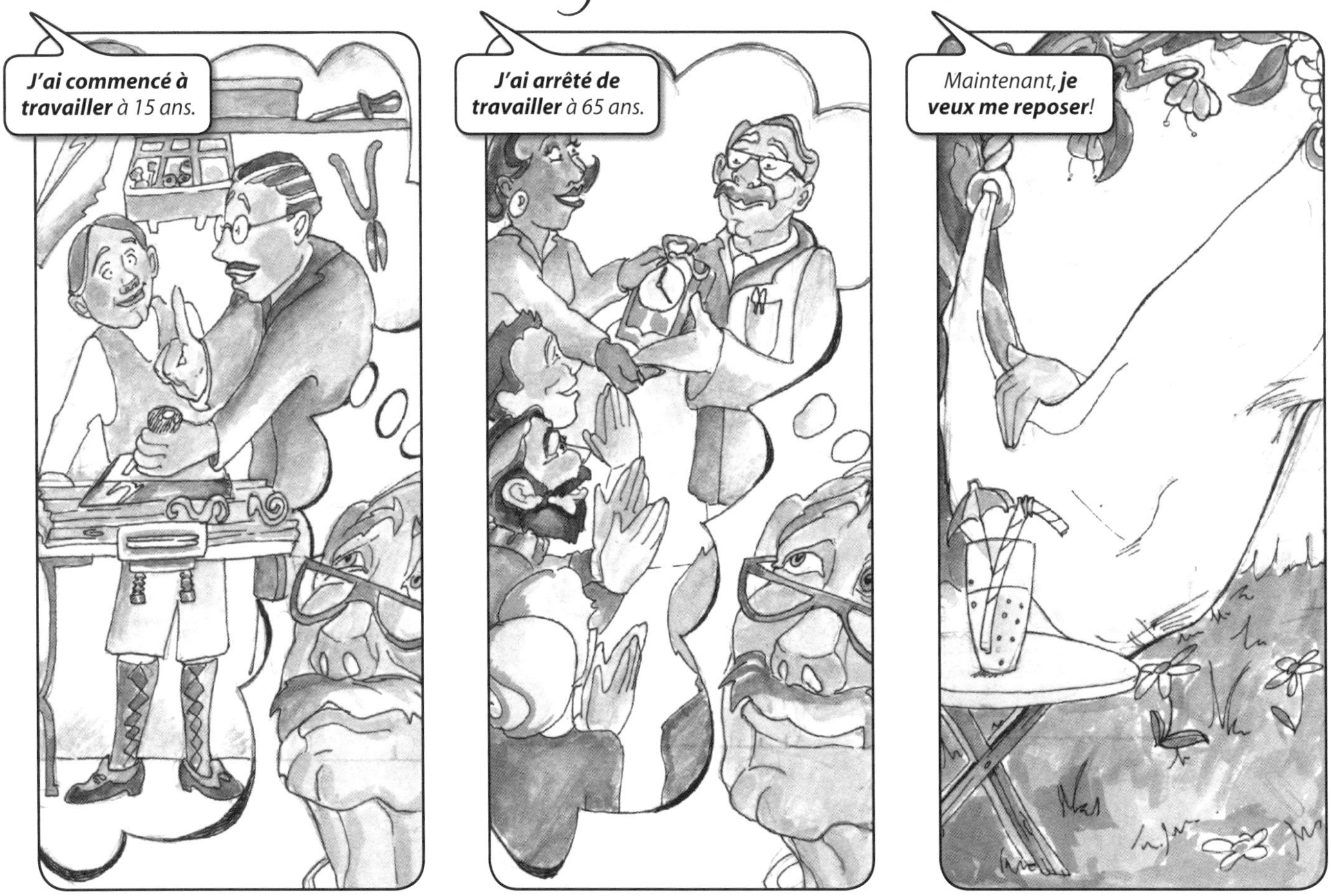

- Some verbs can be followed directly by another verb in the infinitive (the dictionary form of the verb):
  Je veux me reposer. – I want to rest.
- With certain other verbs, you have to use *de*:
  J'ai arrêté de travailler à 65 ans. – I stopped working at 65.
- With a further group of verbs, you have to use *à*:
  J'ai commencé à travailler à 15 ans. – I started working at 15.
- Here are some examples of all three types.

aimer – to like, to love	*arrêter* **de** – to stop	*apprendre* **à** – to learn
préférer – to prefer	*décider* **de** – to decide	*commencer* **à** – to start
vouloir – to want	*essayer* **de** – to try	*continuer* **à** – to carry on
	oublier **de** – to forget	

- Camille talks about her interest in cookery.
  In each gap, decide whether you should add *de*, *à* or nothing at all.

Dans ma famille, nous aimons **1.** Exemple .... *manger. Très petite, j'ai appris* **2.** Exemple ....à.... *faire la cuisine. À 6 ans,*

j'ai commencé **3.** .... *cuisiner des choses simples. Mon pere m'a appris* **4.** .... *faire une omelette. J'ai essayé*

5. .... *faire le dîner pour toute la famille. Maintenant, je préfère* **6.** .... *préparer les desserts.*

Quelquefois, il y a des problèmes! Un jour, j'ai essayé **7.** .... *faire un gâteau. J'ai mis du lait dans une casserole.*

Puis le téléphone a sonné. Je suis sortie et j'ai oublié **8.** .... *fermer la porte de la cuisine. Le chat est entré.*

J'ai continué **9.** .... *bavarder avec mon amie. Quand j'ai arrêté* **10.** .... *parler, trop tard... le chat avait bu le lait.*

J'ai décidé **11.** .... *devenir cuisinière. Un jour, je veux* **12.** .... *travailler dans un restaurant. Mais sans chat.*

Name:

Possession

- The preposition *de* is used to indicate possession. Combined with *le* or *les*, this becomes *du* or *des*.
In English, we use 's':
la voiture de ton père – **your father's car**
le camion de ma mère – **my mother's truck**
le vélo du facteur – **the postman's bike**
la moto des voisins – **the neighbours' motorbike**

- Translate these phrases into French.

1. Théo's books — Exemple: les livres de Théo
2. my grandmother's house ....
3. the teacher's glasses ....
4. the old lady's bag ....
5. our friends' garden ....
6. the neighbours' swimming pool ....
7. the cat's eyes ....
8. my father's flat ....
9. the pupils' homework ....
10. Amélie's croissant ....
11. the visitors' coach ....
12. the little girl's ice cream ....

Name:

pour + infinitive

- The construction *pour* + verb in the infinitive (i.e. verb in the dictionary form) is an easy one to use.
  Elle s'entraîne tous les jours ***pour devenir*** *championne olympique* –
  She trains everyday **to become** an Olympic champion.

- Complete each sentence in French, using *pour* + verb in the infinitive.

Exemple

1. *Je vais en ville* (to meet my friends) pour retrouver mes amis
2. *Elle va à Glasgow* (to learn English) ....
3. *Ils vont à Paris* (to visit museums) ....
4. *Nous rentrons à la maison* (to have lunch) ....
5. *J'allume la télé* (to watch a film) ....
6. *Je monte dans ma chambre* (to read a book) ....
7. *Vous faites du babysitting* (to earn money?) ....
8. *J'ai besoin d'argent* (to buy a PlayStation) ....
9. *Quel train prends-tu* (to go to Nice?) ....
10. *Il faut étudier longtemps* (to become a doctor) ....
11. *Il faut de la vanille* (to make this cake) ....
12. *Elle reste à la maison* (to help her mother) ....
13. *Il prend le bus* (to go home) ....
14. *J'ai besoin de l'ordinateur* (to write a letter) ....

Name:

Link words

- To link ideas, you use <u>link words</u>.
  Nous aimons le soleil, ***alors*** *nous allons sur la Méditerranée.* – We like the sun, **so** we go to the Mediterranean.
  Par contre*, nous n'aimons pas les touristes,* ***donc*** *nous restons dans la tente.* – **On the other hand**, we don't like tourists, **therefore** we stay in the tent.
- Here is a list of the most common link words:

alors – so, therefore	*d'abord* – first of all	*et* – and
bien sûr – of course	*donc* – so, therefore	*mais* – but
car – because	*enfin* – finally	*par contre* – on the other hand
cependant – however	*ensuite* – then	*puis* – then

- Choose which of the three French sentences is the best match for the English sentence.

A As he likes water, he often goes swimming.
1. *J'aime l'eau, mais je vais souvent à la piscine.* ☐
2. *J'aime l'eau, alors je vais souvent à la piscine.* Exemple ☑
3. *J'aime l'eau, puis je vais souvent à la piscine.* ☐

B Although he doesn't like maths, he must do his maths homework.
1. *Je n'aime pas les maths, donc je dois faire le devoir de maths.* ☐
2. *Je n'aime pas les maths, puis je dois faire le devoir de maths.* ☐
3. *Je n'aime pas les maths, mais je dois faire le devoir de maths.* ☐

C The first thing to do to become a footballer is to train everyday.
1. *Pour devenir footballeur, par contre il faut s'entraîner tous les jours.* ☐
2. *Pour devenir footballeur, d'abord il faut s'entraîner tous les jours.* ☐
3. *Pour devenir footballeur, bien sûr il faut s'entraîner tous les jours.* ☐

D It is true she doesn't like fruit, but she does eat a little.
1. *Je n'aime pas les fruits; cependant, j'en mange un peu.* ☐
2. *Je n'aime pas les fruits, alors j'en mange un peu.* ☐
3. *Je n'aime pas les fruits, car j'en mange un peu.* ☐

E She does sport with Marion when she sees her.
1. *Je vois souvent Marion; d'abord, nous faisons du sport ensemble.* ☐
2. *Je vois souvent Marion; bien sûr, nous faisons du sport ensemble.* ☐
3. *Je vois souvent Marion et nous faisons du sport ensemble.* ☐

F At last, Élodie has agreed to go out with Paul.
1. *J'ai téléphoné à Élodie. Ensuite, elle veut bien sortir avec moi.* ☐
2. *J'ai téléphoné à Élodie. Enfin, elle veut bien sortir avec moi.* ☐
3. *J'ai téléphoné à Élodie. Cependant, elle veut bien sortir avec moi.* ☐

G She will travel, but first she will take her exams.
1. *Je vais passer mes examens, et ensuite, je vais voyager.* ☐
2. *Je vais passer mes examens, car je vais voyager.* ☐
3. *Je vais passer mes examens, mais je vais voyager.* ☐

H He eats fish, but he doesn't touch meat.
1. *Je mange du poisson; par contre, je ne touche pas à la viande.* ☐
2. *Je mange du poisson; donc, je ne touche pas à la viande.* ☐
3. *Je mange du poisson, car je ne touche pas à la viande.* ☐

Name:

quand, si and parce que

- You can write more complex sentences using *quand* (when), *parce que* (because) and *si* (if). In front of *il*, *si* becomes *s'*.
Pourquoi? ***Parce que*** *la rivière grossit,* ***quand*** *il pleut.* – Why? **Because** the river swells, **when** it rains.
S'*il y a de l'orage, elle grossit très vite.* – **If** there is a thunderstorm, it swells very quickly

- Write answers in French to the questions. Write full sentences.

1. *Que vas-tu faire si tu réussis à ton examen?* — *partir en Corse*
Exemple: Si je réussis à mon examen, je vais partir en Corse.
2. *Où est-ce qu'on mange quand il fait beau?* — *sur la terrasse*
3. *Pourquoi est-ce que la boulangerie est fermée?* — *le boulanger – en vacances*
4. *Qu'est-ce qu'on fait si la voiture tombe en panne?* — *appeler un garage*
5. *Que font les touristes, quand ils arrivent?* — *visiter la cathédrale*
6. *Pourquoi est-ce que Clément et Julien sont partis?* — *prendre le train dans vingt minutes*
7. *Que va dire Alexandra si sa mère téléphone?* — *expliquer le problème*
8. *Où vont les musiciens quand il pleut?* — *jouer dans le théâtre*
9. *Pourquoi est-ce qu'il n'y a pas d'aéroport à Santa-Maria?* — *ville trop petite*
10. *Que faites-vous si le bateau n'arrive pas?* — *retourner à l'hôtel*

Name:

Cardinal numbers

- It would be simpler if the French for numbers like 70 and 90 followed the Belgian and Swiss way, *septante* and *nonante*, which is much closer to the English 'seventy' and 'ninety'. Instead, you have to remember *soixante-dix* and *quatre-vingt-dix*. Here is a reminder of how numbers are formed in French:

1	*un*
2	*deux*
3	*trois*
4	*quatre*
5	*cinq*
6	*six*
7	*sept*
8	*huit*
9	*neuf*
10	*dix*
11	*onze*
12	*douze*
13	*treize*
14	*quatorze*
15	*quinze*
16	*seize*
17	*dix-sept*
18	*dix-huit*
19	*dix-neuf*
20	*vingt*
21	*vingt et un*
22	*vingt-deux*
30	*trente*
31	*trente et un*
40	*quarante*
50	*cinquante*
60	*soixante*
70	*soixante-dix*
71	*soixante et onze*
72	*soixante-douze*
80	*quatre-vingts*
81	*quatre-vingt-un*
82	*quatre-vingt-deux*
90	*quatre-vingt-dix*
91	*quatre-vingt-onze*
92	*quatre-vingt-douze*
100	*cent*
101	*cent un*
200	*deux cents*
201	*deux cent un*
1000	*mille*
1999	*mille neuf cent quatre-vingt-dix-neuf* **OR** *dix-neuf cent quatre-vingt-dix-neuf*

- Amounts of money often have to be written out in words, as well as in numbers. Write out the amounts on these cheques.

1. Banque de France — Fait à: .... — Payez contre ce chèque: **Exemple** trois cent soixante-treize euros .... — À: .... — Le: .... — **373 €**

2. Banque de France — Fait à: .... — Payez contre ce chèque: .... — À: .... — Le: .... — **495 €**

3. Banque de France — Fait à: .... — Payez contre ce chèque: .... — À: .... — Le: .... — **778 €**

4. Banque de France — Fait à: .... — Payez contre ce chèque: .... — À: .... — Le: .... — **584 €**

5. Banque de France — Fait à: .... — Payez contre ce chèque: .... — À: .... — Le: .... — **831 €**

6. Banque de France — Fait à: .... — Payez contre ce chèque: .... — À: .... — Le: .... — **292 €**

Name:

Ordinal numbers

- The French word game called ***charade*** uses ordinal numbers.
  *Mon **premier** est un oiseau bavard.* – The **first** (syllable) is a talkative bird. (answer: *pie*, 'magpie')
  *Mon **deuxième** est une grosse souris.* – The **second** (syllable) is a large mouse. (answer: *rat*, 'rat')
  *Mon **troisième** est dans la pain.* – The **third** (syllable) is in bread. (answer: *mie*, 'soft part of bread')
  *Mon **quatrième** est un nombre pair.* – The **fourth** (syllable) is an even number. (answer: *deux*, 'two')
  Mon tout est un monument d'Égypte. – The whole (word) is a monument in Egypt. (answer: *pyramide*, 'pyramid')

- This is how ordinal numbers are formed:

The ordinal number for 1 is irregular:	*un*	*le premier/la première*
From 2, just add *–ième* to the number, dropping the final *–e* if necessary:	*deux*	*le/la deuxième*
	trois	*le/la troisième*
	quatre	*le/la quatrième*
Note what happens to 5 and 9:	*cinq*	*le/la cinq**u**ième*
	neuf	*le/la neu**v**ième*
Finally, numbers from 21 ending in *–un* are regular:	*vingt et un*	*le/la vingt et unième*
	trente et un	*le/la trente et unième*

- Re-write the phrases with an ordinal number.

1. *2 – la rue à droite* — **Exemple** la deuxième rue à droite
2. *4 – la semaine de vacances* ....
3. *41 – le concurrent dans la course* ....
4. *22 – l'étage de l'immeuble* ....
5. *12 – le mois de l'année* ....
6. *95 – son anniversaire* ....
7. *57 – la victime de l'accident* ....
8. *7 – le livre de Harry Potter* ....
9. *1 – la guerre mondiale* ....
10. *79 – la ville de France* ....

Name:

Date

- Dates always follow the same pattern: article (+ day) + number + month:
  Je suis née ***le lundi vingt-neuf février****.* – I was born on **Monday**, **February 29th**.
  Je fête mon anniversaire ***le premier mars****.* – I celebrate my birthday **on March 1st**.
- Ordinary numbers (cardinal numbers) are used, except for the first day of the month:
  le mardi premier mars – **Tuesday**, **March 1st**

- Write out the circled dates.

mai

lundi	mardi	mercredi	jeudi	vendredi	samedi	dimanche
(8)	9	10	(11)	12	13	14
15	(16)	17	18	19	20	(21)
(22)	23	24	25	(26)	27	(28)
29	30	(31)				

juin

lundi	mardi	mercredi	jeudi	vendredi	samedi	dimanche
			(1)	2	(3)	4
5	6	(7)	8	(9)	10	11

1. **Exemple** le lundi huit mai
2. ....
3. ....
4. ....
5. ....
6. ....
7. ....
8. ....
9. ....
10. ....
11. ....
12. ....

Time

- Here are some useful time phrases.

le lundi – on Mondays
lundi – on Monday
à 10 heures – at 10 o'clock
de 14 heures à 16 heures – from 2pm to 4pm
à Pâques – at Easter
en mai – in May
en 2005 – in 2005
au 19ème siècle – in the 19th century

- Anthony talks about his favourite holiday. Complete the time phrases.

J'adore les vacances au Club Atlantique. J'y passe deux semaines **1.** ....Exemple: à.... *Noël. Je vais à Fadiou, au Sénégal.*

2. .... *20ème siècle, c'était un petit village de pêcheurs. Mais* **3.** .... *2004, il y a beaucoup de tourisme.*

4. .... *décembre, il fait chaud et il ne pleut pas à Fadiou. Tous les matins* **5.** .... *9 heures, je fais du ski nautique.*

6. .... *midi, on déjeune. L'après-midi,* **7.** .... *1 heure* **8.** .... *3 heures, je me repose.* **9.** .... *samedi, il y a un barbecue et une disco sur la plage.* **10.** .... *dimanche, il y a des excursions dans des parcs ou des réserves.*

J'espère retourner à Fadiou **11.** .... *2005,* **12.** .... *Pâques.* **13.** .... *mars ou avril, il fait toujours beau.*

Name:

Quantity

- Here are several ways of talking about quantity.
C'est ***à cinq kilomètres d'ici***. – It is **five kilometres from here**.
une lettre de 50 grammes – **a 50-gram letter**
Ça coûte/Ça fait 50 centimes*. – **It costs/That's 50 cents**.
30 litres d'*essence* – **30 litres of** petrol
200 grammes du *raisin* – **200 grams of** grapes
un kilo de *pommes de terre* – **a kilo of** potatoes
un morceau de *fromage* – **a piece of** cheese

* Remember that one euro is divided into 100 *centimes*.

* *le colis* – parcel
* *l'alimentation* – food shopping

- Audrey and Kévin's mother sends them shopping. Write out the quantities in the gaps.

Audrey et Kévin, pouvez-vous faire quelques courses? D'abord, l'alimentation. Vous pouvez aller à l'épicerie,*

1. Exemple à 500 mètres d'ici *(500 m), ou au supermarché,*

2. .... *(2 km). J'ai besoin de* **3.** ....

(eau minérale – 6 l) et de **4.** .... *(pommes – 2 kg). Je voudrais aussi*

5. .... *(viande – 400 g) et* **6.** ....

(framboises – 200 g). Il me faut aussi **7.** .... *(gruyère – petit morceau).*

Aussi, pouvez-vous passer à la poste? C'est **8.** .... *(300 m). J'ai plusieurs choses*

à poster: **9.** .... *(3 lettres – 20 g) et* **10.** ....

(colis – 1 kg). Je pense que l'alimentation,* **11.** .... *(10 euros), et les lettres*

et le colis, **12.** .... *(8 euros). Voici 20 euros.*

Answers

1

Voici le piano, les lits, les fauteuils, la cuisinière, le frigo, le lave-vaisselle, les armoires, l'ordinateur, les rideaux, la moquette, les étagères, la baignoire. Voici un piano, des lits, des fauteuils, une cuisinière, un frigo, un lave-vaisselle, des armoires, un ordinateur, des rideaux, une moquette, des étagères, une baignoire.

2

1. *animaux*
2. *chevaux*
3. *mains*
4. *genoux*
5. *hôpitaux*
6. *magazines*
7. *journaux*
8. *gâteaux*
9. *bonbons*
10. *bateaux*
11. *clowns*
12. *enfants*
13. *bureaux*
14. *cadeaux*
15. *idées*

3

1. *Je veux envoyer des lettres – mais je n'ai pas d'enveloppes.*
2. *Je voudrais faire des crêpes – tu as de la farine?*
3. *Je n'ai pas de livres parce que je n'ai pas de devoirs.*
4. *Dans mon thé, je prends du lait, mais pas de sucre.*
5. *On fait de l'allemand et de l'espagnol, mais on ne fait pas de latin.*
6. *Il faut de la patience et du courage pour ce travail.*
7. *Dans la ville, il y a des églises, mais pas de cathédrale.*
8. *Les végétariens mangent du fromage, mais pas de viande.*
9. *Elle a de l'argent, mais elle n'a pas d'amis.*
10. *Je cherche des chaussures, mais je ne veux pas de chaussures chères.*

4

1. *prochaines*
2. *idéale*
3. *écossais*
4. *verts*
5. *variés*
6. *écossaises*
7. *élégantes*
8. *sympa*
9. *français*
10. *vrai*
11. *hanté*
12. *propres*
13. *polluées*
14. *simple*
15. *pratique*

5

1. *nouvelle*
2. *ancienne*
3. *affreuse*
4. *ennuyeux*
5. *neuves*
6. *blanches*
7. *belles*
8. *bonne*
9. *gentilles*
10. *paresseuses*
11. *végétarienne*
12. *grosses*
13. *délicieux*
14. *heureuse*

6

1. *Chère Maman*
2. *de bonnes vacances*
3. *une ville agréable*
4. *une plage propre*
5. *de longues promenades*
6. *du vieux port*
7. *les jolies boutiques*
8. *des vêtements chers*
9. *des films ennuyeux*
10. *de bons repas*
11. *un petit appartement*
12. *un appartement ancien*
13. *ma propre chambre*
14. *une famille sympa*
15. *des vacances fantastiques*

7

1. *Le mont Blanc est plus haut que Ben Nevis.*
2. *Le mont Blanc est moins haut que l'Everest.*
3. *Le pingouin est aussi rapide que le saumon.*
4. *Le Shinkansen est plus rapide que le TGV.*
5. *Le Flying Scotsman est moins rapide que le TGV.*
6. *Une Ferrari est aussi chère qu'une Rolls-Royce.*
7. *En ski, les Norvégiens sont meilleurs que les Espagnols.*
8. *La France est plus grande que la Grande-Bretagne.*
9. *La Grande-Bretagne est moins grande que les États-Unis.*
10. *L'espagnol est aussi difficile que le français.*
11. *Le climat en Italie est plus chaud que le climat en Irlande.*
12. *Le climat en Islande est moins chaud que le climat en Irlande.*
13. *Le tigre sibérien est aussi rare que le panda.*
14. *En base-ball, le Canada est meilleur que la France.*

8

1. *Le guépard est l'animal le plus rapide.*
2. *Le bateau est le moyen de transport le moins dangereux.*
3. *Le vin français est le meilleur vin d'Europe.*
4. *Harry Potter est le livre pour enfants le plus célèbre.*
5. *En Écosse, on trouve les plages les moins polluées de Grande-Bretagne.*
6. *Le colibri est le plus petit oiseau du monde.*
7. *Le train est le moyen de transport le moins fatigant.*
8. *La reine Elizabeth est la femme la plus importante d'Angleterre.*
9. *L'autruche est l'oiseau le moins intelligent.*
10. *Sydney est la plus grande ville d'Australie.*
11. *Les élèves préfèrent les professeurs les moins sévères.*
12. *Jéricho est la ville la plus ancienne du monde.*

9

A
1. *cet appareil-photo*
2. *cette caméra*
3. *ces téléphones portables*
4. *cet ordinateur*

B
1. *cet immeuble*
2. *ces maisons*
3. *cette église*
4. *ce château*

C
1. *ces graffiti*
2. *cet incendie*
3. *cet accident*
4. *cet orage*

D
1. *cette pomme*
2. *ces raisins*
3. *ce melon*
4. *cet abricot*

10

1. *chaque*
2. *chaque*
3. *quelques-uns*
4. *quelques*
5. *chaque*
6. *quelques*
7. *chaque*
8. *quelqu'un*
9. *quelque chose*
10. *quelqu'un*
11. *quelques*
12. *quelque chose*

11

1. *mon*
2. *sa*
3. *mon*
4. *notre*
5. *son*
6. *votre*
7. *ma*
8. *notre*
9. *ta*
10. *leur*
11. *leur*
12. *ta*
13. *ma*
14. *ton*

12

1. *vos, nos, vos*
2. *ses*
3. *mes, tes*
4. *leurs*
5. *mes, vos, nos*
6. *vos, leurs*
7. *mes, ses*

13

1. *plus près que, le plus près*
2. *plus vite que, le plus vite*
3. *moins souvent que, le moins souvent*
4. *mieux que, le mieux*
5. *moins loin que, le moins loin*
6. *plus facilement que, le plus facilement*

14

1. *Comment*
2. *Où*
3. *Où*
4. *Pourquoi*
5. *À quelle heure*
6. *Combien de temps*
7. *Quand*
8. *Comment*
9. *Combien*
10. *Combien*
11. *pourquoi*

15

1. *Hier*
2. *tôt*
3. *tard*
4. *Aujourd'hui*
5. *D'abord*
6. *En même temps*
7. *Ensuite*
8. *récemment*
9. *en retard*
10. *Plus tard*
11. *enfin*
12. *Demain*
13. *de bonne heure*
14. *tout de suite*
15. *déjà*

16

Suggested Answers

1. *tous les jours*
2. *Quelquefois/Parfois/Souvent*
3. *jamais*
4. *En général/Généralement*
5. *quelquefois/parfois*
6. *jamais*
7. *Quelquefois/Parfois*
8. *quelquefois/parfois*
9. *souvent*
10. *toujours*
11. *toujours*
12. *souvent*
13. *encore*
14. *souvent*
15. *encore*
16. *jamais*

17

A **1c**, **2d**, **3a**
B **1d**, **2c**, **3a**
C **1d**, **2c**, **3b**
D **1b**, **2a**, **3d**

18

1. *Damien habite à Paris depuis 1995.*
2. *Lucie a cassé sa montre il y a trois jours.*
3. *Depuis le 1er janvier, Benjamin fait de la natation.*
4. *Natacha apprend l'allemand depuis deux ans.*
5. *Il y a deux mois, Valentin a visité la National Gallery.*
6. *Depuis 2002, Juliette fait de la danse.*
7. *Pablo a acheté une moto il y a un an.*
8. *Léa fait de l'équitation depuis cinq ans.*
9. *Djamel vit en France depuis 1999.*
10. *Il y a six mois, Sophie est allée à Disneyland Paris.*
11. *Adrien habite chez son père depuis deux ans.*
12. *Il y a une semaine, Lauren a perdu son portable.*

19

Suggested Answers

1. *Je n'aime pas cette soupe: il y a trop de sel.*
2. *Le dimanche matin, il n'y a pas beaucoup de voitures sur la route.*
3. *Il pleut beaucoup: prends ton parapluie.*
4. *Il pleut trop: je ne sors pas!*
5. *Le cours de photographie est annulé: il n'y a pas assez de participants.*
6. *Si tu as trop chaud, enlève ton pull.*
7. *L'hiver en Tunisie, il ne fait pas très froid: on peut se baigner.*
8. *Ahmed est un peu malade, mais ce n'est pas grave: il va à l'école.*
9. *Saïda est trop malade pour aller à l'école.*
10. *Baptiste est à l'hopital aujourd'hui, parce qu'il est très malade.*
11. *Le lundi matin, il y a beaucoup de voitures sur la route.*
12. *Le lundi matin, il y a trop de voitures sur la route, alors je prends le train.*
13. *J'aime un peu/assez la physique, mais je préfère les maths: j'aime beaucoup l'algèbre.*
14. *Il est mauvais, ton gâteau: il n'y a pas assez de sucre.*

20

1a, **2b**, **3a**, **4a**, **5a**, **6b**, **7b**, **8a**, **9b**, **10a**, **11b**, **12b**

21

jeter

1. *les chaussures*
2. *le chapeau*
3. *la ceinture*
4. *les chaussettes*
5. *la casquette*

aimer/garder

1. *le pull*
2. *la veste*
3. *les collants*
4. *le blouson*
5. *les gants*

donner à Emmaüs

1. *la chemise*
2. *les baskets*
3. *le bonnet*
4. *la jupe*
5. *le T-shirt*

22

Pupils should tick:
1, **6**, **8**, **10**

23

1b, **2a**, **3b**, **4a**, **5a**, **6b**, **7a**, **8a**, **9b**, **10b**, **11a**, **12a**

24

1. *Moi*
2. *nous*
3. *moi*
4. *eux*
5. *nous*
6. *Eux*
7. *lui*
8. *nous*
9. *nous*
10. *eux*
11. *toi*
12. *Toi*
13. *moi*

25

1. *chez elle*
2. *sans lui*
3. *chez eux*
4. *pour moi*
5. *avec lui*
6. *de nous*
7. *pour elle*
8. *pour nous/moi*
9. *pour vous/toi*
10. *à toi*
11. *à côté de lui*

26

1. *la moto*
2. *les livres*
3. *les tables*
4. *la montre*
5. *le crayon*
6. *mon ordinateur*
7. *les haricots*
8. *les baskets*
9. *le casque*

27

1. *Qui*
2. *Qu'est-ce que*
3. *Qu'est-ce qui*
4. *Qui*
5. *Qui*
6. *Qu'est-ce qu'*
7. *Qui*
8. *Qui*
9. *Qui*
10. *Qu'est-ce qui*
11. *Qu'est-ce que*
12. *Qu'est-ce que*
13. *Qu'est-ce que*
14. *Qui*

28

A **1c**, **2e**, **3d**, **4a**
B **1d**, **2a**, **3c**, **4e**
C **1c**, **2e**, **3a**, **4d**

29

1. *suis*
2. *êtes*
3. *est*
4. *sont*
5. *êtes*
6. *est*
7. *sont*
8. *sommes*
9. *es*
10. *suis*
11. *sont*
12. *sont*
13. *est*
14. *est*
15. *sont*

30

1. *as*
2. *ai*
3. *ont*
4. *a*
5. *a*
6. *avons*
7. *a*
8. *ont*
9. *a*
10. *as*
11. *a*
12. *a*
13. *avez*
14. *avons*
15. *a*
16. *ai*
17. *ont*
18. *a*
19. *a*

31

A
1. *Elle achète une veste.*
2. *Je préfère les chaussures noires.*
3. *Tu essaies le pantalon bleu?*
4. *Tu aimes le pull rouge?*

B
1. *Elle préfère les bottes en hiver.*
2. *Je paie avec ma carte.*
3. *On mange souvent à la cafétéria.*
4. *Il porte une chemise amusante.*

C
1. *Tu essaies la veste noire.*
2. *Elle paie avec sa carte.*
3. *Il travaille à la cafétéria.*
4. *Tu achètes tes chaussures ici?*

32

1. *achètent*
2. *travaillons*
3. *préférez*
4. *commençons*
5. *nageons*
6. *préparent*
7. *ferment*
8. *mangeons*
9. *achetez*
10. *achetons*
11. *décident*
12. *lavez*

33

1. *choisis*
2. *finissent*
3. *remplissons*
4. *remplis*
5. *finit*
6. *choisis*
7. *remplis*
8. *finit*
9. *remplissez*
10. *finis*
11. *choisissent*
12. *finis*

34

1. *Vous rendez le livre à la bibliothèque?*
2. *Elle vend des glaces sur la plage?*
3. *Je descends à la prochaine station.*
4. *Vous répondez aux questions du prof?*
5. *Je perds souvent de l'argent.*
6. *Tu entends la musique à la radio?*
7. *Nous répondons au téléphone.*
8. *Ils entendent un bruit dans le moteur.*
9. *Nous attendons les vacances avec impatience.*
10. *Tu vends aussi des vêtements?*
11. *Elles attendent le train de 10 heures 17.*
12. *Il descend à la cave.*

35

1. *Tu t'appelles Karim, comme mon père.*
2. *Il se repose dans le hamac.*
3. *Il se réveille vers 4 heures.*
4. *Pendant les vacances, je m'amuse bien.*
5. *Je me baigne dans la Méditerranée.*
6. *On se lève tous les jours à midi.*
7. *Je me promène dans les vieilles rues.*
8. *Tu t'intéresses aux bateaux?*
9. *Non, je m'intéresse à la pêche.*
10. *Tu te disputes avec ta sœur?*
11. *Non, je m'entends bien avec elle.*
12. *Elle se couche tous les jours à minuit.*

36

1. *nous nous écrivons*
2. *vous vous voyez*
3. *nous nous retrouvons*
4. *ses parents se disputent*
5. *ils s'appellent*
6. *vous vous intéressez*
7. *nous nous baignons*
8. *nous nous promenons*
9. *qui s'intéressent*
10. *vous vous disputez*
11. *vous vous entendez*
12. *nous nous amusons*

37

1. *veux*
   peux
2. *pouvez*
   peux
3. *voulez*
   dois
4. *veux*
   devez
5. *veut*
6. *peut*
   doit
7. *veux*
   veulent
8. *veux*
   doit
9. *veulent*
   peuvent
10. *doivent*
    peuvent

38

A	**1.**	*allons*	**d**
	2.	*viennent*	**b**
	3.	*savent*	**a**
B	**1.**	*va*	**b**
	2.	*sais*	**c**
	3.	*revient*	**a**
C	**1.**	*vais*	**c**
	2.	*sait*	**b**
	3.	*revenons*	**a**
D	**1.**	*sait*	**d**
	2.	*devient*	**a**
	3.	*va*	**c**

39

1. *comprennent*
2. *prends*
3. *comprends*
4. *comprend*
5. *prennent*
6. *comprenons*
7. *apprends*
8. *apprend*
9. *prend*
10. *prennent*
11. *apprenez*
12. *apprend*

40

1. *part*
2. *partent*
3. *partent*
4. *sort*
5. *courent*
6. *courent*
7. *partons*
8. *court*
9. *cours*
10. *sortent*
11. *cours*
12. *court*
13. *courent*
14. *sort*

41

Pupil's answers may vary.

42

1. *décrit*
2. *dites*
3. *recevons*
4. *reçois*
5. *disent*
6. *écrivent*
7. *écrit*
8. *dit*
9. *décrit*
10. *recevez*
11. *recevons*
12. *disons*
13. *écrivez*
14. *écris*

43

1 (**2** and **3**)

a) *Il/Mon père met (les décorations sur le sapin de Noël.)*
b) *Elles/Ma mère et ma sœur mettent (les décorations sur le sapin de Noël.)*
c) *Tu mets (les décorations sur le sapin de Noël.)*
d) *Vous mettez (les décorations sur le sapin de Noël.)*

4, 5, 6

a) *il/elle ouvre*
b) *ils/elles ouvrent*
c) *tu ouvres*
d) *vous ouvrez*

7, 8

a) *il/elle boit*
b) *ils/elles boivent*
c) *tu bois*
d) *vous buvez*

44

1. *Nous vivons dans une petite maison.*
2. *Je connais les voisins.*
3. *Ils voient les montagnes.*
4. *Du haut de la tour, on voit la mer.*
5. *Vous connaissez/Tu connais le musée, n'est-ce pas?*
6. *Vous vivez/Tu vis très près de la plage.*
7. *Les flamants vivent à côté de la rivière.*
8. *Je vois les bateaux tous les matins.*
9. *Les vieux habitants du village connaissent tout le monde.*
10. *Elle connaît toutes les plantes.*
11. *Tu vois/Vous voyez des coquillages rares.*
12. *Le vieil homme vit seul.*

45

1c, 2b, 3a, 4b, 5c, 6a, 7b, 8c

46

1. *Manon ne s'amuse pas tout le weekend.*
2. *Elle ne se repose jamais le dimanche.*
3. *Elle ne se lève pas à 10 heures du matin.*
4. *Elle ne s'intéresse plus aux émissions de télé.*
5. *Elle ne se promène jamais dans les magasins en ville.*
6. *«Je ne me couche pas à 9 heures du soir.»*
7. *Manon et son frère ne se disputent jamais.*
8. *«Je ne m'entends pas bien avec ma meilleure amie.»*
9. *«Tu ne te baignes jamais à la plage.»*
10. *Manon et ses amis ne se retrouvent plus au café.*
11. *«Tes amis et toi, vous ne vous voyez pas le soir.»*
12. *«Ma correspondante et moi, nous ne nous écrivons plus tous les jours.»*

47

1. *Allez-vous au cinéma?*
   Vous allez au cinéma?
   Est-ce que vous allez au cinéma?
2. *Est-ce un film de James Bond?*
   C'est un film de James Bond?
   Est-ce que c'est un film de James Bond?
3. *Passe-t-il à l'Odéon?*
   Il passe à l'Odéon?
   Est-ce qu'il passe à l'Odéon?
4. *Est-il pour les moins de 18 ans?*
   Il est pour les moins de 18 ans?
   Est-ce qu'il est pour les moins de 18 ans?
5. *Emmenez-vous Mickaël?*
   Vous emmenez Mickaël?
   Est-ce que vous emmenez Mickaël?
6. *Prenez-vous la voiture?*
   Vous prenez la voiture?
   Est-ce que vous prenez la voiture?
7. *Y a-t-il de l'essence dans la voiture?*
   Il y a de l'essence dans la voiture?
   Est-ce qu'il y a de l'essence dans la voiture?
8. *Rentrez-vous avant minuit?*
   Vous rentrez avant minuit?
   Est-ce que vous rentrez avant minuit?

48

1. *Pourquoi est-ce que tu n'appelles pas?*
   Why don't you call?
2. *Pourquoi ne vient-il pas?*
   Why isn't he coming?
3. *Qu'est-ce qu'elle ne mange pas?*
   What doesn't she eat?
4. *Qu'est-ce qui ne coûte pas cher?*
   What isn't expensive?
5. *Qui est-ce qui ne part pas en vacances?*
   Who doesn't go away on holiday?
6. *Est-ce que ce livre n'est pas trop dur?*
   Isn't this book too hard?
7. *Est-ce que vous ne prenez pas votre vélo?*
   Aren't you taking your bike?
8. *N'allez-vous pas au cinéma ce soir?*
   Aren't you going to the cinema tonight?
9. *Qui n'a pas ses affaires de sport?*
   Who hasn't got their sport kit?
10. *Pourquoi ne laissez vous pas ce travail?*
    Why don't you leave this job?

49

1. *Vous aimez*
2. *tu achètes*
3. *Tu veux*
4. *tu ne comprends pas*
5. *tu penses*
6. *toi*
7. *s'il vous plaît*
8. *Vous voulez*
9. *vous avez*
10. *vous allez*
11. *vous voulez*
12. *s'il te plaît*
13. *tu bois*
14. *s'il vous plaît*

50

1. *Il faut prendre de l'aspirine.*
2. *Il faut téléphoner au garage.*
3. *Il faut repeindre les classes.*
4. *Il faut travailler dur.*
5. *Il faut se coucher tôt.*
6. *Il faut installer des poubelles.*
7. *Il faut faire la vaisselle.*
8. *Il faut aller chez le coiffeur.*
9. *Il faut acheter un cadeau.*
10. *Il faut ouvrir la fenêtre.*
11. *Il faut manger.*
12. *Il faut faire les courses.*

51

1. *a fêté*
2. *ont organisé*
3. *a invité*
4. *a préparé*
5. *a fini*
6. *ai choisi*
7. *a perdu*
8. *ai décoré*
9. *ai rempli*
10. *a attendu*
11. *a regardé*
12. *ont commencé*
13. *a pleuré*
14. *a répondu*
15. *avons parlé*
16. *avons mangé*
17. *avons passé*

52

A
1. *a eu*
2. *ont couru*
3. *a dû*
4. *ont bu*

B
1. *a cru*
2. *as eu*
3. *ai conduit*
4. *avons couru*

C
1. *ont cru*
2. *as conduit*
3. *a dû*
4. *avez bu*

53

1. *Monsieur Michaud a dit «Fermez vos livres de maths».*
   Mr Michaud said, 'Close your maths books.'
2. *Monsieur Michaud a écrit les questions au tableau.*
   Mr Michaud wrote the questions on the board.
3. *Les élèves ont lu les questions au tableau.*
   The pupils read the questions on the board.
4. *Renaud a mis le livre de maths sur ses genoux.*
   Renaud put his maths book on his knees.
5. *Renaud a ouvert le livre de maths.*
   Renaud opened the maths book.
6. *Renaud a pu voir la bonne réponse.*
   Renaud could see the correct answer.
7. *Les élèves ont fait le devoir de maths.*
   The pupils did the maths test.
8. *Monsieur Michaud a dit «Vous avez écrit les réponses?»*
   Mr Michaud said, 'Have you written the answers?'
9. *Monsieur Michaud a lu le devoir de Renaud.*
   Mr Michaud read Renaud's work.
10. *Monsieur Michaud a écrit «Tu as fait le devoir seul, Renaud?»*
    Mr Michaud wrote, 'Did you do the work on your own, Renaud?'
11. *Renaud a dit «Non, j'ai ouvert le livre».*
    Renaud said, 'No, I opened the book.'
12. *Renaud a été puni.*
    Renaud was punished.

54

1. *ai appris*
2. *ai vu*
3. *ai voulu*
4. *ont vu*
5. *ont suivi*
6. *ai compris*
7. *a pris*
8. *ai reçu*
9. *ont ri*
10. *ont ri*
11. *ai ri*
12. *ai reçu*

55

1. *est tombé*
2. *ai entendu*
3. *suis descendue*
4. *ai regardé*
5. *ai vu*
6. *ont appelé*
7. *suis sortie*
8. *sont arrivés*
9. *sont montés*
10. *ont jeté*
11. *est sorti*
12. *est resté*
13. *n'est pas mort*
14. *est parti*
15. *n'est pas revenu*

56

1. *Je me suis réveillée à 5 heures du matin.*
2. *Je me suis levée à 6 heures.*
3. *Jonathan s'est réveillé à 6 heures.*
4. *Jonathan s'est levé à 7 heures.*
5. *Nous nous sommes disputés, parce qu'il est paresseux.*
6. *Je me suis lavée dans la neige.*
7. *Nous nous sommes promenés en traîneau à chien.*
8. *Les chiens se sont baignés dans l'eau glacée.*
9. *Je me suis reposée dans un igloo.*
10. *Nous nous sommes amusés dans la neige.*
11. *Jonathan s'est couché à 11 heures.*
12. *Je me suis couchée à minuit.*

57

1. *j'étais*
2. *il y avait c'était*
3. *nous étions*
4. *il y avait*
5. *on avait*
6. *nous avions*
7. *avaient*
8. *j'étais*
   j'avais
9. *nous avions*
10. *avait*
11. *était*
12. *nous étions*

58

1. *faisais*
2. *faisait*
3. *faisions*
4. *faisiez*
5. *faisais*
6. *faisais*
7. *faisaient*
8. *faisait*
9. *faisaient*
10. *faisait*

59

1N, **2**P, **3**N, **4**P, **5**P
6N, **7**N, **8**P, **9**N, **10**P,
11P, **12**N, **13**P, **14**N

60

1. *je marchais / j'ai vu*
2. *je buvais / j'ai entendu*
3. *a reçu / elle travaillait*
4. *est arrivée / préparait*
5. *allait / est tombée*
6. *tu faisais / tu as perdu*
7. *est entré / dormait*
8. *est tombé / était*
9. *a mangé / avait faim*
10. *êtes partis / étiez fatigués*
11. *se baignait / a vu*
12. *ai commencé / j'avais*

61

A
1. *Nous allons mettre des fleurs dans le jardin.*
2. *Le professeur va lire les devoirs.*
3. *Mes parents vont faire les magasins.*
4. *Vous allez partir en vacances.*
5. *Tu vas apprendre l'espagnol.*
6. *Elles vont recevoir des cadeaux.*
7. *Je vais prendre le train.*
8. *Le docteur va venir chez nous.*

B
1. *Élodie va commencer le piano.*
2. *Vous allez vous lever à 7 heures du matin?*
3. *Je vais manger une pizza.*
4. *Nous allons essayer le patinage sur glace.*
5. *Tu vas monter à la tour Eiffel?*
6. *Il va aimer ce chanteur.*
7. *Kévin et Alexandre vont jouer au tennis.*
8. *Ils vont se baigner avant le déjeuner.*

62

Quand je serai grand, je serai astronaute.
D'abord, j'irai à l'université et j'étudierai la mécanique et l'aéronautique.
Ensuite, j'entrerai dans l'armée de l'air.
On me donnera un bel uniforme, et mes parents seront contents!
Je pense que je ferai beaucoup de sport, et de l'entraînement tous les jours.
Je me préparerai très bien.
Quand on me choisira pour une mission, j'espère aller sur la Lune, et peut-être sur Mars.

63

1. Elle voudrait/aimerait écouter ce disque.
2. Mes parents voudraient/aimeraient une maison plus petite.
3. Je voudrais/J'aimerais visiter Paris.
4. Nicolas voudrait/aimerait un VTT.
5. Nous voudrions/aimerions sortir samedi soir.
6. Est-ce que vous voudriez/aimeriez/tu voudrais/aimerais venir avec moi?
7. On voudrait/aimerait/Nous voudrions/aimerions connaître la fin de l'histoire.
8. Ils/Elles voudraient/aimeraient partir en vacances.
9. Clara voudrait/aimerait être médecin.
10. Tu voudrais/aimerais/Vous voudriez/aimeriez devenir millionnaire?
11. Elles/Ils voudraient/aimeraient une voiture neuve.
12. Il voudrait/aimerait du sucre dans son café.

64

1. Je pensais que tu avais compris.
2. Elle avait marché longtemps et elle était fatiguée.
3. J'ai écouté le disque que tu m'avais recommandé.
4. Ils avaient étudié le chinois avant de partir en Chine.
5. Thomas a pleuré parce qu'il avait cassé sa petite voiture.
6. Romain avait réussi à son examen, alors il a reçu un cadeau.
7. J'avais travaillé dur et je voulais partir en vacances.
8. Anaïs m'avait donné son numéro, mais je l'ai perdu.
9. Vous avez lu le livre que je vous avais donné?
10. Ils avaient perdu leur chemin, alors ils sont entrés dans le café.
11. Sophie a dit qu'elle avait gagné à la Loterie.
12. Elles ont regardé le film qui avait eu un Oscar.

65

1. Choisis un pantalon!
2. Finis le devoir de maths!
3. Montez dans le taxi!
4. Asseyez-vous!
5. Lave-toi!
6. Mange ta viande!
7. Attends le bus!
8. Réponds au professeur!
9. Couchez-vous!
10. Mets les couverts sur la table!
11. Fais ton lit!
12. Baignez-vous dans la piscine!

66

1. Ne prenez pas l'ascenseur!
2. Explique-moi le problème!
3. Ne vous promenez pas sur la plage!
4. Répondez-lui!
5. Ne le prends pas!
6. Ne lui achète pas de roses!
7. Ne lui donne pas de cravate!
8. Téléphone-lui vite!
9. Achète-moi ce CD, s'il te plaît!
10. Ne te baigne pas dans la rivière!
11. Ne leur parlez pas!
12. Donne-le-moi!

67

1. Je suis payé dix euros pour laver la voiture.
2. Si vos devoirs sont faits, vous pouvez sortir.
3. La robe est achetée; maintenant je cherche des chaussures.
4. Si la clef est perdue, qu'est-ce qu'on va faire?
5. En général, les repas sont préparés à la cuisine.
6. La cantine est repeinte en jaune.
7. Est-ce que tu es choqué par ce film?
8. Si les travaux sont finis, l'école peut ouvrir.
9. Les bambous sont mangés par les pandas.
10. Le château est surtout visité l'été.
11. Les rivières sont polluées par l'usine.
12. Les lettres sont distribuées le matin à 10 heures.

68

1. étant
2. ayant
3. sachant
4. connaissant
5. étant
6. dormant
7. habitant
8. pensant
9. voyant
10. voulant

69

1. J'ai 18 ans
2. j'ai envie
3. ont besoin
4. nous avons de la chance
5. nous n'avons pas faim
6. nous n'avons pas soif
7. Nous n'avons pas souvent froid/chaud
8. ont faim
9. elles ont soif
10. elles ont mal
11. ont peur
12. Tu as tort
13. ça a l'air
14. je n'ai pas peur
15. j'ai raison

70

1. Quand il fait beau, Clémence fait du sport.
2. Quand il fait chaud, ma grand-mère fait de la natation.
3. Quand il fait mauvais, Anthony fait de la flûte.
4. Quand il fait du soleil, nous faisons de l'athlétisme.
5. Quand il fait du vent, vous faites du deltaplane?
6. Quand il fait froid, mes amies font les magasins.
7. Quand il fait chaud, tu fais du cricket?
8. Quand il fait du soleil, Jonathan fait du bateau.
9. Quand il fait beau, je fais du camping.
10. Quand il fait mauvais, Mathilde fait du piano.
11. Quand il fait froid, Léo et Coralie font du ski.
12. Quand il fait du vent, nous faisons du cerf-volant.

71

1. jouer au foot
2. jouer au rugby
3. jouent au hockey
4. jouent au basket
5. jouent au tennis
6. jouent au ping-pong
7. jouer de la batterie
8. jouent du piano
9. jouent de la guitare
10. joue de la flûte
11. jouer du synthé
12. jouent aux échecs
13. joue au golf
14. joue au cricket

72

1. au Canada
2. au Québec
3. dans une petite ville
4. À Saint-Philémon
5. à Saint-Philémon
6. en France
7. à Paris
8. Dans une grande ville
9. en Belgique
10. à Bruxelles
11. au Luxembourg
12. en Angleterre
13. aux États-Unis
14. à New York
15. à Seattle
16. à Montréal
17. En Amérique

73

1. dans
2. Sous
3. entre
4. sur
5. dans
6. Devant/Derrière
7. Dehors
8. derrière
9. dedans
10. vers
11. Dehors
12. sous

74

A
1. Il y a un lac près de Saint-Médard.
2. On peut pique-niquer au bord du lac.
3. Si on loue un bateau, on peut visiter l'île au milieu du lac.
4. On peut se promener autour de l'île.
5. Au fond du lac, on peut voir des poissons.

B
1. À côté/En face du lac, il y a un café.
2. En face/À côté du café, il y a une route.
3. Au bout de la route, il y a une tour ancienne.
4. C'est intéressant d'aller jusqu'à la tour.

C
1. La tour n'est pas loin du lac: 500 mètres.
2. En haut de la tour, il y a un drapeau.
3. En bas de la tour, il y a une porte.
4. De l'autre côté de la tour, on voit de grands arbres.

75

A
1. J'y vais en train.
2. J'y vais en bateau.
3. J'y vais en moto.

B
1. J'y vais en voiture.
2. J'y vais à pied.
3. J'y vais en avion.

C
1. J'y vais en car.
2. J'y vais en bus.
3. J'y vais en vélo.

D
1. J'y vais en avion.
2. J'y vais en vélo.
3. J'y vais en bus.

76

1. *après*
2. *avant/pour*
3. *sauf*
4. *sans*
5. *par*
6. *chez*
7. *sans*
8. *chez*
9. *contre*
10. *Pour*
11. *Après*
12. *par*

77

1. *la seule à*
2. *contente de*
3. *facile d'*
4. *possible d'*
5. *impossible de*
6. *prête à*
7. *la première à*
8. *dangereux de*
9. *important d'*
10. *la dernière à*
11. *prête à*
12. *facile de*

78

1. *nous aimons manger*
2. *j'ai appris à faire*
3. *j'ai commencé à cuisiner*
4. *m'a appris à*
5. *j'ai essayé de*
6. *je préfère préparer*
7. *j'ai essayé de faire*
8. *j'ai oublié de fermer*
9. *J'ai continué à bavarder*
10. *j'ai arrêté de parler*
11. *J'ai décidé de devenir*
12. *je veux travailler*

79

1. *les livres de Théo*
2. *la maison de ma grand-mère*
3. *les lunettes du professeur*
4. *le sac de la vieille dame*
5. *le jardin de nos amis*
6. *la piscine des voisins*
7. *les yeux du chat*
8. *l'appartement de mon père*
9. *les devoirs des élèves*
10. *le croissant d'Amélie*
11. *le car des visiteurs*
12. *la glace de la petite fille*

80

1. *Je vais en ville pour retrouver mes amis.*
2. *Elle va à Glasgow pour apprendre l'anglais.*
3. *Ils vont à Paris pour visiter les musées.*
4. *Nous rentrons à la maison pour déjeuner.*
5. *J'allume la télé pour regarder un film.*
6. *Je monte dans ma chambre pour lire un livre.*
7. *Vous faites du babysitting pour gagner de l'argent?*
8. *J'ai besoin d'argent pour acheter une PlayStation.*
9. *Quel train prends-tu pour aller à Nice?*
10. *Il faut étudier longtemps pour devenir médecin.*
11. *Il faut de la vanille pour faire ce gâteau.*
12. *Elle reste à la maison pour aider sa mère.*
13. *Ile prend le bus pour rentrer chez lui.*
14. *J'ai besoin de l'ordinateur pour écrire une lettre.*

81

A2, B3, C2, D1, E3, F2, G1, H1

82

1. *Si je réussis mon examen, je vais partir en Corse.*
2. *Quand il fait beau, on mange sur la terrasse.*
3. *La boulangerie est fermée parce que le boulanger est en vacances.*
4. *Si la voiture tombe en panne, on va appeler un garage.*
5. *Quand ils arrivent, les touristes visitent la cathédrale.*
6. *Clément et Julien sont partis parce qu'ils prennent le train dans vingt minutes.*
7. *Si sa mère téléphone, Alexandra va expliquer le problème.*
8. *Quand il pleut, les musiciens jouent dans le théâtre.*
9. *Il n'y a pas d'aéroport à Santa-Maria parce que la ville est trop petite.*
10. *Si le bateau n'arrive pas, nous retournons à l'hôtel.*

83

1. *trois cent soixante-treize euros*
2. *quatre cent quatre-vingt-quinze euros*
3. *sept cent soixante-dix-huit euros*
4. *cinq cent quatre-vingt-quatre euros*
5. *huit cent trente et un euros*
6. *deux cent quatre-vingt-douze euros*

84

1. *la deuxième rue à droite*
2. *la quatrième semaine de vacances*
3. *le quarante et unième concurrent dans la course*
4. *le vingt-deuxième étage de l'immeuble*
5. *le douzième mois de l'année*
6. *son quatre-vingt-quinzième anniversaire*
7. *la cinquante-septième victime de l'accident*
8. *le septième livre de Harry Potter*
9. *la première guerre mondiale*
10. *la soixante-dix-neuvième ville de France*

85

1. *le lundi huit mai*
2. *le jeudi onze mai*
3. *le mardi seize mai*
4. *le dimanche vingt et un mai*
5. *le lundi vingt-deux mai*
6. *le vendredi vingt-six mai*
7. *le dimanche vingt-huit mai*
8. *le mercredi trente et un mai*
9. *le jeudi premier juin*
10. *le samedi trois juin*
11. *le mercredi sept juin*
12. *le vendredi neuf juin*

86

1. *à*
2. *Au*
3. *en*
4. *En*
5. *à*
6. *À*
7. *de*
8. *à*
9. *Le*
10. *Le*
11. *en*
12. *à*
13. *En*

87

1. *à 500 mètres d'ici*
2. *à deux kilomètres d'ici*
3. *six litres d'eau minérale*
4. *deux kilos de pommes*
5. *400 grammes de viande*
6. *200 grammes de framboises*
7. *un petit morceau de gruyère*
8. *à 300 mètres d'ici*
9. *trois lettres de 20 grammes*
10. *un colis d'un kilo*
11. *ça fait/coûte 10 euros*
12. *ça fait/coûte 8 euros*